G000135296

Making Sense in Sign

Parents' and Teachers' Guides

Series Editor: Professor Colin Baker, *University of Wales, Bangor, Wales, Great Britain*

Other Books in the Series
The Care and Education of a Deaf Child: A Book for Parents
    Pamela Knight and Ruth Swanwick
Dyslexia: A Parents' and Teachers' Guide
    Trevor Payne and Elizabeth Turner
Guía para padres y maestros de niños bilingües
    Alma Flor Ada and Colin Baker
A Parents' and Teachers' Guide to Bilingualism
    Colin Baker
Second Language Students in Mainstream Classrooms
    Coreen Sears

Other Books of Interest
The Care and Education of Young Bilinguals: An Introduction to Professionals
    Colin Baker
Encyclopedia of Bilingualism and Bilingual Education
    Colin Baker and Sylvia Prys Jones

Please contact us for the latest book information:
Multilingual Matters, Frankfurt Lodge, Clevedon Hall,
Victoria Road, Clevedon, BS21 7HH, England
http://www.multilingual-matters.com

PARENTS' AND TEACHERS' GUIDES 6
Series Editor: Colin Baker

Making Sense in Sign
A Lifeline for a Deaf Child

Jenny Froude

'Today language abandoned me. I could not find the word for a simple object – a commonplace familiar furnishing. For an instant, I stared into a void. Language tethers us to the world; without it we spin like atoms. Later, I made an inventory of the room – a naming of parts: bed, chair, table, picture, vase, cupboard, window, curtain. Curtain. And I breathed again.

I have put my faith in language …

I control the world so long as I can name it. Which is why children must chase language before they do anything else, tame the wilderness by describing it, challenge God by learning His hundred names.'

Penelope Lively (*Moon Tiger*)

MULTILINGUAL MATTERS LTD
Clevedon • Buffalo • Toronto • Sydney

Dedicated to:

- Tom who delights and humbles me in equal measure, who needed so much, demanded so little and gave back so much more than I expected or deserved.
- Family, friends and professionals who inspired, encouraged, supported or prayed. They are many, they are special, and they know who they are (indeed many have kindly allowed me to name them!).

Library of Congress Cataloging in Publication Data
Froude, Jenny
Making Sense in Sign: A Lifeline for a Deaf Child/Jenny Froude.
Parents' and Teachers' Guides: 6
1. Froude, Thomas. 2. Deaf children–Great Britain–Biography. 3. Froude, Jenny.
4. Parents of deaf children–Great Britain–Biography. 5. Deaf–Means of
communication–Great Britain. I. Title. II. Series.
HV2717.F76 F76 2003
362.4'2'083–dc21   2002015682

British Library Cataloguing in Publication Data
A catalogue entry for this book is available from the British Library.

ISBN 1-85359-629-9 (hbk)
ISBN 1-85359-628-0 (pbk)

Multilingual Matters Ltd
UK: Frankfurt Lodge, Clevedon Hall, Victoria Road, Clevedon BS21 7HH.
USA: UTP, 2250 Military Road, Tonawanda, NY 14150, USA.
Canada: UTP, 5201 Dufferin Street, North York, Ontario M3H 5T8, Canada.
Australia: Footprint Books, PO Box 418, Church Point, NSW 2103, Australia.

Copyright © 2003 Jenny Froude. The right of Jenny Froude to be identified as the author of this work has been asserted by her in accordance with the Copyright Designs and Patents Act 1988.

All rights reserved. No part of this work may be reproduced in any form or by any means without permission in writing from the publisher.

Typeset by Archetype-IT Ltd (www.archetype-it.com)
Printed and bound in Great Britain by the Cromwell Press Ltd.

Contents

Introduction vii
Acknowledgements viii

1   The Time of Crisis 1
2   Deafness may Result 12
3   Take My Hands and Let Them Move 24
4   Channels of Communication 39
5   Good Times – Bad Times 51
6   Coping and Caring 71
7   Growing Up 80
8   Sound or Silence? 98
9   Staying Strong 108
10 The Big Adventure 118
11 Language for Life 128
12 Borneo and Beyond 145
13 What is Deaf? 153
14 Paths to Understanding 160

Appendix 1: A Letter to a Deaf Son 'Yellow is a
            Lovely Word to See' 167
Appendix 2: A Second Letter to a Deaf Son 169
Appendix 3: Some Useful Addresses 171
Appendix 4: Glossary 175

References 177
Index 179

Introduction

Tom Froude's story is first of all simply a good read in itself. The account of how he and his family have responded to what seemed to be a disaster without remedy, and with repercussions to come later, will absorb anyone who enjoys reading biography.

But the book is so much more than a good yarn, and written readably. In the form of a story, true and true to life, told clearly and accurately, but with passion and sensitivity, Jenny and Tom offer help, advice and hope to an incalculable number of people. Without being in the least sanctimonious they speak not only to those who are deaf, but also to those who care for deaf people, those who teach them, those who employ them, those who work with them, and those who serve them in a wide variety of ways. If a conspiracy of those human resources which we all have deep within ourselves and those divine resources which are ours by faith in God can in one life bring good out of evil, then it must be possible again and again. If Tom, why not me? If Jenny, why not me?

I was once privileged to minister to Tom. Now he ministers to me. I myself have now become partially deaf and well understand what that means in practical terms: a struggle to continue to work or play, to understand what people are saying, wondering what they are laughing at, and increasingly depending on captions on television and loops in the theatre. We who experience such disabilities need the encouragement which Tom's story can give. Indeed, we all, whatever our abilities or lack of them, need often to be reminded that among the joys of being human is to experience love, and hope, and kindness, serving others and being served. If the human race were free from all pain and disability we should not be living in a 'brave new world' but existing in a timid and tired world without that joy which is the fruit of faith, hope and love.

Tom's overwhelming desire has been, in his own words in his self awareness book, to 'help people'. That desire has been, and will continue to be, richly fulfilled, because his story is now shared with many readers, and will influence the daily lives of many more.

✠ David Ballarat,
Australia, March 2002

Acknowledgements

All family photographs are © J. Froude, except those on pp. 47 and 48 which are © The Kentish Times and which are reproduced with their kind permission.

The photograph of the booklet shown on p. 99 is reproduced by kind permission of the Director of Education, London Borough of Bromley.

The author also gratefully acknowledges the kind permission of Allen Lane (The Penguin Group UK) to quote from Penelope Lively's book, *Moon Tiger* (1988).

Chapter 1

The Time of Crisis

The depths of human affection and kindness are not plumbed without a crisis. (Jack Ashley, 1973)

I don't know whether you know what an enormous volume of prayers and goodwill goes out to you from everyone who knew you at *Woman's Weekly*. I hope it helps you a little. (Gaye Allen, Home Editor)

I shall never forget the August 1980 Bank Holiday. All weekend I had been irritable and depressed for no apparent reason. Strange, since the weather was good, our three children all well and PMT isn't a problem when one's breast-feeding and the hormones aren't back to normal. But I couldn't shake off a feeling of impending doom. It even prompted me to search a cupboard, desperately trying to find an article from *Good Housekeeping* magazine which had haunted me some years previously, about a mother whose first child died shortly after birth. I found it and read it again, to this day I have no idea why, and hoped my husband wouldn't notice the tears which flowed just as they had done the first time I saw it.

On the Monday we went to visit a neighbour. Thomas had a slightly runny nose. Joan took him on her lap with the words 'Goodness me, Thomas, five months old and this is the first time I've had a real cuddle'. He smiled in his usual merry way.

All afternoon he slept in his pram in the garden. He had refused a feed at lunchtime. I put it down to teething. In the evening he started to whimper and lay on my shoulder. I still put it down to teething but I did look up meningitis in the medical dictionary. At that time it was not an illness given a high profile; most of us were blissfully unaware of it. But I had recently heard of a baby, born to a couple who had almost given up hope of a child of their own, who had developed meningitis at the age of six weeks and was dangerously ill. The story haunted me, especially since we ourselves had been married for 11 years before our first child was born and had known something of the heartache of apparent infertility. I couldn't get that baby out of my mind, even though the family were not local and were unknown to me personally.

1

Adoring glances from Matthew and Daniel for newborn Tom

Since his birth, Thomas had always slept in a Liberty-lawn-lined wicker crib beside our bed. He was just outgrowing it and I was preparing him for the transition to the big cot in his own room by putting him in there at bedtime and bringing him in to us for a feed and to sleep the remainder of the night in our room. It had only happened once and already I had felt a shudder go through me at the sight of the empty crib when I went to bed. It had made me think what it must feel like to have a cot death; the sense of separation was so appalling.

But on that fateful Bank Holiday evening I put Thomas to bed beside us in the old way. He woke for a feed at 5 a.m. Three hours later he was pale, unhappy and couldn't bear to be touched. I rang the doctor and put Thomas in the pram downstairs, beside me. It was a beautiful, hot morning. I envisaged a sun-filled day in the garden for us all.

Our GP, a gruff, ex-army doctor, approaching retirement, called. He rang Farnborough Hospital immediately and asked to speak to the paediatrician. I don't remember what he said, apart from 'I don't like the noise he's making'. An ambulance was summoned to take us straightaway.

'Is it meningitis?', I asked. 'Could be, could be', he muttered, 'there's a lot of it about'.

Matthew and Daniel, six and five years old, were left with their grannie who, luckily, had a flat at the top of our house. I grabbed a cardigan for me

Secure in a loving family – one of the few
early snapshots

Communicating with a doting dad

Tom's happy smile at 2 months

and a shawl for the baby and we left. It was to be three weeks before we returned home together.

Meningitis Confirmed

During the journey and on arrival Tom's eyes hardly left my face but as soon as we got into the isolation ward he started having fits. It was eleven days since his second immunisation against diptheria and tetanus but the registrar felt there was no connection with his present state. I can only cling to the hope that she was correct. A lumbar puncture revealed pneumo-coccal meningitis. His sparse, blonde hair was shaved and lines inserted to carry the vital antibiotics. I had to break the appalling news to my husband, John, at work.

By the evening, in great discomfort, I asked if there was somewhere I could go to express my milk. I remember the consultant paediatrician stopping in her tracks. She felt we were so very, very unlucky to have a breastfed baby in this state. And, because of the nature of Tom's illness, my milk was of no use to the Special Care Baby Unit. The only time I'd had milk to spare and it had to be poured away.

In my shock I am sure most of my questions were silly ones. How long would we be in hospital? Could the bacteria have lain dormant for some time, undetected, remembering the particularly persistent and violent headache and feverish feelings I'd suffered only two weeks after his birth? The gravity of the situation had not really sunk in. We were told that Thomas was a very sick little boy and that the next 48 hours would be critical. Irrationally, I began to feel I had somehow wished this dreadful illness on him, simply by my preoccupation with that other, unknown infant whose meningitis had so preyed on my mind.

A camp bed was made up for me in the tiny room. I must have dozed off eventually, only to be awoken in the middle of the night by the registrar expressing her concern about Tom. She had called a colleague over from Sydenham Children's Hospital; Thomas was fitting dreadfully. I asked if these fits would lead to brain damage in the future? His grave reply – 'I don't think we should be thinking too much about the future tonight' – tore at my heart. I wanted to phone my husband but was told there was no need, yet . . .

Later that night, as I sat expressing more milk in an empty room along the corridor, I heard footsteps and then the voice of a nurse asking the words I'd been dreading I'd hear all day: 'Mother, has this baby been baptised?'

Oh, the relief, despite my despair, of being able to answer in the affirmative. Thomas's baptism at Beckenham Parish Church had been a joyous occasion some two months previously, attended by family, godparents, some of our dearest friends. The sun had shone. Thomas's behaviour had been just perfect. We had just had the photographs developed. The only thing that had struck me about them was how frail he looked in his long white gown. How slender his neck. How like photos of his elder brother, Matthew, at the same age. And Matthew has a mental handicap for no known reason. Were we going to see the same with Thomas?

And then I remembered Matthew's teacher in his Special Opportunity class picking up the tiny Thomas and hearing her say to him 'Well, I shan't be having you in my class I can see', so bright were his eyes and so interested his gaze even at a few weeks old. And the man who was to become Matthew's head-teacher at his junior school seeing Thomas at only two weeks old, at a National Childbirth Trust talk he gave and to which I'd struggled expressly to hear him, remarking how lucky Thomas was.

But all that positive feedback was suddenly in the past. Just part of my questioning heart during those long, lonely, anxious hours. Such silly things bugged me. The fact that, despite my best intentions, I had taken so few snapshots of Thomas's early weeks and that, in my haste to get home

Family group after Thomas's baptism, June 1980

with him 48 hours after his birth, I had left behind his tiny hospital cot label. At the time the latter had felt like a little disappointment; now it assumed the giant proportions of an ominous portent. I could also see, in my mind's eye, the dear little shiny green mac' and sou'wester I'd bought so prematurely for him in the summer sales, to fit a two year old. Such vain things that had charmed me and must now be sacrificed.

And with a pang, as I sat there I saw Thomas in relation to others. He was my baby and the umbilical cord seemed so recently to have been cut that I could only think in terms of us two. Suddenly I saw him as John's son, the boys' brother, grandson to two doting grandmothers and I realised he was not my personal possession but part of us _all_. My plea, 'Oh Thomas, _please_ don't die; I love you so much' sounded selfish when I realised he was loved and needed by us all. But at that moment it didn't help; it just made it all the worse. It wasn't just a personal grief. The enormity of the loss we were _all_ likely to face overwhelmed me.

Back in Tom's room I eventually drifted into sleep towards dawn. It was a mistake. When I awoke, as the hospital stirred into action at 6 a.m., I thought it had all been a bad dream. I was wrong. The prostrate form in the cot convinced me it was all too horribly real.

Our rector, the Reverend David Silk, just back from a Spanish holiday, came at a friend's request and anointed Thomas with holy oil while we joined in prayers at his side. (He told me years later he had gone straight home to his wife and, in answer to her unspoken query, had shaken his head, hopelessly.) John brought Thomas's baptism candle to comfort me. It showed that he had passed 'from darkness into light' but could anything be darker than these hours?

After Father David's visit, despite constant fits, Thomas got through the day. His eyes were shut, his head seemed huge, his navel (which had never been the neatest) seemed swollen. How I longed to pump my strength back into him, as I had done for those nine happy months. I looked at the head which was so desperately paining him. 'God be in his head and in his understanding', I prayed.

The nurses would regularly proffer a damp cotton swab on a stick to refresh his parched mouth. He would seek out for it avidly, like a newborn rooting at the breast, but oh how it reminded me of a sponge soaked in vinegar and offered to another dying man . . .

By the following afternoon Thomas seemed to come alive a little. To our innocent eyes his colour appeared better. The nurses let me hold him briefly and put him to the breast. I was terrified. In two days I had forgotten how it felt to hold him. And the lines from his poor head got in the way. But we took it as a good sign. The 48 hours were almost over.

It was a disappointment when the consultant paediatrician didn't share our pleasure. She still seemed worried.

An agency nurse was on special duty that night. For the first time I felt uneasy about the staffing. I could sense that the nurses going off duty shared my concern. Thomas had been 'specialled' and cot-nursed with the minimum of handling. He had not been left for a second since our arrival but when I returned from the bathroom I found him alone. I awoke in the night to his cries and found the nurse cradling him in her arms and crooning. It broke my heart; I knew how *any* movement increased his agony.

In the early morning the agency nurse was gone. A personal crisis at home had resulted in her immediate departure and, to my relief, a familiar staff nurse was on duty.

That morning found Thomas apparently no worse. The 48 hours had passed. Outside his room I saw the doctor brought over specially on the first night, who had then gently prepared me for the worst. This time he said confidently 'he'll be alright now'. And I believed him . . .

In the afternoon I was expressing milk when John arrived. His face was ashen.

'What's the matter?' I asked. 'I've just seen Tom', was all he said. We knew then that things were *not* improving. We were told that the consultant wanted to see us. After what seemed like an eternity she took us into the office and asked how we were coping. Would I like Valium? I remember asking if Thomas was brain dead. We were told he was comatose. I knew this doctor was trying to prepare us for his death but she did add that sometimes things happen that we don't always understand. If only she knew, that was all we were hoping and praying for. Prayers were what I needed, not Valium.

She explained that a bed was ready for our baby in intensive care at Guy's Hospital in London if his condition made it necessary to administer even stronger drugs to kill the bacteria since they could, at the same time, depress his respiration. He would have to go on a ventilator. The staff thought we should go home but I couldn't bear the thought of leaving. Outside, the rain poured down and all we heard that afternoon was the wail of ambulance sirens.

The previous day I had been persuaded to pop home at teatime. My mother's face had lit up at her hopeful query 'Does this mean Tom is getting better?' That day I knew she and the boys were preparing a special tea. I couldn't ring anyone to ask for a lift; my grief couldn't be shared or inflicted on anyone else just then and yet I didn't want to leave Tom alone. But in the end John and I did dash home together. It was a wretched journey and I swear there were more prams than usual on the way. Or did it just seem like it?

When we reached home, I couldn't speak. The fire was on, the tea (prepared by the boys) all beautifully laid out. My mother took one look at my face and knew it was not, after all, a time for rejoicing . . .

Before we returned to the hospital, I got the boys ready for bed. Daniel struggled out of a blue and white striped T-shirt that was on the tight side.

'I think I'll have to put this away for Tom', he announced, with the air of a five-year-old who has already earmarked several outgrown things for his baby brother. I froze. I *couldn't* let them go on thinking Thomas would be home again. I took a deep breath and explained that if God couldn't make Thomas better here on earth he would take him to heaven and look after him there for us. But that he would always be our baby and we would always talk about him, never forget him . . . I was aware of a choking sound as John left the room.

'Yes' accepted Daniel, solemnly, 'and he'll come back to us when he's a big daddy, won't he?'

I took a last look at Tom's crib in our room, at his cot with the patchwork cover I'd made him in his nursery. I said goodbye on his behalf. We returned to the hospital.

Thomas was given a brain tap, to relieve the pressure. We weren't allowed near him. We sat locked together in the waiting room as rain cascaded down the windows and tears down my face.

'I can't stand it', I sobbed. But I had to, John had to and, worst of all, poor little Tom had to, too.

To make things even worse on that black Friday most of our favourite nurses went off duty for the weekend. I said goodbye to them, so certain was I that by the time they returned we would have gone home, empty-handed.

Turning Point

Despite everything Thomas got through the night. We didn't go to Guy's. And in the morning, I think towards 6 a.m., he had his last fit. After that the sun shone, the day dawned brightly and, although we didn't believe it then, he was over the worst. His godmother, Anne, and her husband raced down from Kensington as soon as they got my letter. I had unashamedly written to as many people as I could, especially those I knew were blessed with a strong faith. I so wanted their prayers for Thomas and he was named and remembered not only in our own church of St George, Beckenham, but in prayers and masses said in several parts of Kent, Sussex, Essex and Hampshire that weekend. On Sunday, while I was at the service in the little hospital chapel, weeping over the hymn lines 'Does a mother's love cease toward the child she bore?' my midwife came and left a bottle of holy water from Lourdes for us. People were so very thoughtful.

Like another mother before me, I had so much time in those dreadful days to ponder things in my heart. Little events, people, attitudes are crys-tallised for ever in my mind. The nurses who were so supportive to us all, as a family. Who got into trouble for becoming too involved, for ringing up on their off-duty days to check Tom's progress, who pasted bulletins about him on their doors? Where are they now, I wonder, those brilliant young-sters of August 1980? I still think of them and of the part they played in our particular history.

One of our favourites, a little Welsh nurse, was getting married and excitement was in the air. I remember the orchard outside our ward, full of pear trees, and seeing the nurses walking through it, their cloaks blowing in the wind, laughing and talking but, such was the insulation, I could hear no sound. And little did I know then that Tom never would.

And so the days passed. I became aware of the contrast between Tom's pale little body and my almost obscenely tanned hands and arms. It was quite a strain keeping up with the milk supply to be tube fed to him but, apart from praying, it was all I could do for him. There was one night when I went staggering up the corridor, bleary-eyed, only to find that it was impossible to produce anything! I was desolate until I realised I'd misread the time and it was less than an hour since the last expressing. Just as I was becoming exhausted Thomas was pronounced fit enough to feed direct (and continued to do so until he was two years and two months).

Words of one of our favourite Barbra Streisand songs haunted me in those days. 'Jenny Rebecca' is a lovely celebration of childhood, full of lines like 'swings to be swung on, trees to be climbed up, days to be young on, toys you can wind up, grass to be lying on . . . love to be giving, dreams to be daring for, *'long as you're living'*. Would Thomas live to do any of those things? And, if he survived, what? I think we knew he could not come through this nightmare unscathed. Something so devastating just had to leave its mark. But what would that mark be? We feared a mental handicap most – that Tom would not know us.

I looked up 'meningitis' in a child's health book. 'Deafness may result', it said. But whenever Thomas had an injection, a blood transfusion or other treatment, I would hold him as best I could and, of course, talk to him all the while. 'He knows your voice', the nurses would exclaim. It didn't occur to me he knew nothing but the *look* of me, the *feel* of me, the *smell* of me. Whenever we had to leave him briefly we put the 'Hush-a-Bye Baby' cassette (RCA Red Seal RK 42751) playing in a cassette player in his cot. How I loved that music from the days when he and I lay together recovering our strength after his birth. To this day I can't hear Pachelbel's 'Canon' and Fauré's 'Pie Jesu' without a pang. In retrospect, the fact that the tape was compiled by Michele Clements, a research fellow in audiological medicine, makes it all the more extraordinary.

As Thomas got stronger, the days became colder. I had to change my sundress for something warmer. His brothers returned to their respective schools armed with letters from me explaining the traumas we'd suffered, although both of them coped wonderfully well, thanks to their amazing grandmother who, even at 85, was able to be a tower of strength to us all. They never once complained at my absence, never clung or cried when, later on, they visited us in hospital. Until the time came for Tom to be off all the drips and monitors I didn't want them to even peep through the window. If he died I didn't want them to remember him in that state. What a contrast it would have been to their first sight of him after his birth when, visiting me in hospital, they had peered round the door and when I, wanting them to understand their own place in the birth events, pointed out the bed I'd occupied after Matthew's delivery and the other after Daniel's, had been delighted by the latter's reaction. Wide-eyed, he'd gazed around the remaining beds and whispered 'and which bed were you in after you had Daddy?' In Bickley isolation ward I felt far removed from that 'Mother Earth' figure four-year-old Daniel had obviously felt me to be that night!

Early Suspicions

During our last week in Farnborough Hospital, the nurse I had found most supportive asked me, quite casually, if I would have expected

Thomas to have turned to a certain noise. He was lying in his cot, with his back to us. 'Only he doesn't respond when I come in the door', she explained. I realise now that this was just the beginning . . .

But, of course, naïve as we were, we had no idea how to check a baby's hearing in such circumstances. We would drop things and people within Tom's vision would react. He would appear to turn to the sound. It was to be the first and possibly the last time that others' automatic responses to noise would give him the clues he needed to fool us. We told ourselves brightly, confidently – too confidently – that it would be all right. The consultant paediatrician guessed but said it could be a temporary loss.

'Carry on talking to him', she advised, as she discharged him on 16 September, three weeks to the day after our arrival.

Outside it felt very cold, a distinct hint of autumn in the air. Thomas's first summer had ended. Safely. But in silence.

Chapter 2

Deafness May Result

Our gift, when the time came, was perfect in every way. But my faint-hearted faith had led me, despite a deep, inner conviction, to allow medical science to confirm that this would be so (with all that that implies) long months before. Is that why, I have asked myself so often, God so nearly reclaimed his gift after only a few months in our possession, only returning it at the last minute, damaged beyond repair but to us more beautiful and infinitely more precious than ever before?

I wrote those words, anonymously, for our parish magazine after a particularly thought-provoking address one Remembrance Sunday when our then rector, the Reverend Jeremy Saville, touching on abortion, asked his congregation which one of them, so close to Christmas, would willingly throw away an unopened gift?

My third pregnancy was very definitely a planned one, as were both others. It had taken us seven years to conceive our first son, mere months for the second and, although I was approaching 40, I desperately wanted to add to our family. I admit, therefore, that I embarked upon it without a qualm, armed with the knowledge that an amniocentesis test would be available. In the ten months it took before Thomas was conceived, my hitherto comfortable acceptance of such a procedure changed a little and, by the time I knew I was pregnant, I remember walking to the altar rails to Communion feeling sure, deep within me, that this baby was sound. I would refuse a test, I decided.

At the first ante-natal visit a doctor, just within earshot, read my notes and pronounced 'She's a candidate for an amniocentesis'. But to my delight I heard the voice of the sister remonstrating with 'Perhaps you should ask her how she feels about it?' My refusal was on my lips but I did agree to see a genetic adviser and, in view of the fact that twins were suspected, to have an ultrasound scan. And somehow, somewhere along the line I found myself agreeing to the test. My elderly mother was living with us. Our first son had learning disabilities requiring special schooling and it was all too easy to convince myself that I couldn't cope with more problems. But I shall never know if I would have opted for a termination had the test revealed abnormalities. Particularly in the event of Down's Syndrome I like to think I would have been able to cope, armed with the knowledge in advance so that from before the birth I would have been prepared for such a baby. I shall never know for sure, of course, but I do feel I was making bargains with God. A perfect baby or else . . .

When the day for the test arrived I went, ashamedly, to the 11 o'clock Eucharist, somehow feeling that everyone must suspect what I was about to undergo. I prayed so hard that morning that God would not let me spill this baby, knowing as I did the risks the test carried and having Louis MacNeice's 'Prayer before Birth' (1966) in my mind.

> 'I am not yet born; O fill me
> With strength against those who would freeze my humanity'

and

> ' . . . like water held in the hands would spill me'.

But Thomas wasn't spilt and I came home from Guy's Hospital and spent the weekend in bed to ensure his safety as much as I could. And I have to confess it was the best birthday present I could have, just prior to my fortieth, to read the letter telling me the chromosome count appeared normal. The tears were of relief although even then, such was my guilt, I told myself something would probably go wrong during labour instead. I didn't want to know the sex of the baby as I felt that that, at least, should be God's own lovely secret left undisturbed until delivery – and anyway I enjoyed the few months of thinking I might be the mother of that longed-for daughter at last!

My pregnancy progressed beautifully, with none of the problems experienced by my younger friends, and Thomas arrived a week late (the longest week of my life) and it was only during one particularly bad point in the undrugged, forceps delivery that I remember thinking grimly that it had better be a girl after all this. But nearly nine pounds of furious, lusty baby boy were delivered – and I loved him immediately!

Deep down, I think I had known we were destined to have three sons, especially after that first breathtaking sight of him on the scan at about 14 weeks, when all I could see clearly was his rounded little head and neck which already seemed so dearly familiar, so like the shape of his two brothers'. I stood on London Bridge station afterwards, hugging this special, secret sight to myself in wonder, convinced I'd been privileged to see a little glimpse of heaven that morning.

And heaven it surely seemed in September 1980, to be home with Thomas after his three weeks in the isolation ward. We were armed with

So happy to have their baby brother back!

giant bottles of medicine to prevent any more fits, with folic acid to build him up, and with an appointment for the following week to see the consultant paediatrician. We were clinging to the hope that it was just a little residual inflammation that was affecting Tom's hearing.

Once home it would have been difficult to detect that Thomas had ever been so ill. He had, amazingly enough, not lost weight in hospital and looked as bonny as before. We had seen him slowly come back to life there, gradually awaking to his strange surroundings, finally flirting cheekily with the nurses before we left. He was slow to sit up and was, though we didn't know it then, going to be very late and often clumsy in walking due, I'm sure, to the hearing loss affecting his balance.

We kept our appointment the following week. This time the consultant was no longer hopeful. 'I'm pretty sure he's not hearing that', she said as he made no response to the variety of sounds she produced for him. We could no longer go on pretending . . .

A referral was made to an ENT consultant who duly saw Thomas in early October and confirmed a hearing loss but explained that further, sophisticated tests would be necessary and referred us to the National Hospital for Nervous Diseases in Queen Square, London. However, he did hold out one ray of hope. In ten years' time, he explained, cochlear implants would be available and Thomas's name would go down immediately on a waiting list, to become one of the first to receive one. What wonderful news! We were impressed. It sounded like excellent, 'high tech' stuff to us.

In retrospect it proves how innocent we were, still recovering from the shock of the illness and having no real understanding of deafness and all its implications, especially for a baby too young to have acquired any spoken language. We were, of course, clutching at straws. It gave us something positive and hopeful to tell our shocked families, our friends, *ourselves.*

It may seem strange, even unnatural, that we never shed any tears over Tom's deafness at that time. But this has to be seen in the light of his dreadful illness. We knew only too well the devastation it could have caused and by the time we discovered deafness was the only legacy of the merciless meningitis (or so we thought then) the time for weeping was over. We had had our son restored to us through what seemed little short of a miracle. Not brain damaged, not blinded, not paralysed, only deaf. We couldn't ask for more.

Early Detection of Deafness

I am sure the way in which it was discovered helped, too. It says a lot for that young nurse who first mentioned it so calmly, almost casually, that I had time to come to terms with the idea, before the paediatrician confirmed it. To be told by the team who had been so closely involved with us when saving Tom's life was one thing. To have been discharged (as I know other parents elsewhere have been) with the assurance that all is well, only to return months later with suspicions and be told one is neurotic or over-reacting, before professionals finally have to concede damage has been done, must make the acceptance so much harder. And I think for us, *knowing* why Tom is deaf helps us to explain it to others, as well as to him. Had he been born deaf, for no apparent reason, I think our story could have started very differently.

One's reaction and attitude to deafness must also be coloured by one's previous experience. Sometimes it seemed as if I had been prepared for such close proximity to it. My career in the magazine world had started as junior to the formidable Winifred (Biddy) Johnson (c. 1893–1978), wonderful deaf editor of three top-selling women's magazines (*Woman's Weekly, Woman & Home* and *My Home*). She was famous for simply switching off her hearing aid when meetings with the management weren't going her way!

The film 'Mandy' had made a big impression on me in the 1950s. I still remember the way she turned to the light from the bedroom doorway and nearly fooled her parents into believing she could hear and, alongside my mother, I certainly shed a few tears when the television programme 'Blue

Peter' launched one of its famous appeals, on behalf of deaf children, in the 1970s. And when, as secretary of the local National Childbirth Trust, I had to arrange for a social worker to come and talk on the subject of deafness in children, I recall being mortified that out of 500 members only three of us bothered to attend. My paragraph in the next newsletter about 'falling on deaf ears' was written in disgust – and that was some years before Tom was born. After he became deaf it was not until I was confronted with a deaf-blind manual language chart in a book I'd borrowed that I remembered how, some 28 or so years earlier, as a Red Cross cadet, I had regularly taken out an elderly deaf-blind lady in St Leonards-on-Sea, spelling directly on to her hands and finding great difficulty in understanding her strained speech. And lastly there was my own mother, whose deafness was the sort that comes with advancing years. The agonies of embarrassment I used to suffer when, ensconced in her favourite front seat of a bus, she would talk in such strident tones that the rest of the passengers were party to our entire conversation! To my shame I had, shortly before Tom's illness, repri-manded her for talking so loudly coming down the stairs that she awoke the sleeping baby in the pram in the hall. Never again would that be a cause for concern.

But when Tom's deafness was discovered there was only one deaf person I had in my mind, the thought of whom gave me so much confi-dence and, I'm sure, was instrumental in helping my acceptance.

I met severely deaf Lynda an hour after I gave birth to Daniel, her own daughter having been born a few days previously. She was the only person in a busy ward to notice that I was in a state of shock and when, finally, the unexpected post-natal complications were such that I had to have emergency surgery at midnight and a recovery room to myself, it meant we had little time to continue our brief acquaintance. A willowy blonde, I was convinced, through my pain and plummeting blood pressure, that her accent was Scandinavian. It was some time before I realised she was *deaf*. The irony of it was that, five years later, our mutual friends from the local nursery school were too embarrassed to tell her when Thomas lost his hearing. That proved what she herself had often told me ruefully, that her deafness is her life; it's other people who turn it into a *handicap* for her.

Quite recently Lynda has confessed to me that she was horrified to find early on how my feelings on the diagnosis were influenced by our friend-ship. Other friends were telling her they couldn't understand my reaction and calm acceptance of the situation and Lynda, of course, realised that the prognosis for Tom was far more serious than *her* hearing loss. For my part I still feel anything, however naïvely I latched on to it, that helped us through those early, vulnerable months was a bonus. And by the time I was more aware of the implications other help was at hand to give us a confidence that has remained.

It has been said that there are five factors which contribute to the distress of parents confronted with newly diagnosed deafness in their child. These are ignorance, a feeling of distance, a poor image of deafness, the real difficulties that deaf people face and having a lot of hearing expectations.

Well, we certainly were ignorant, but in those early, baby days it was impossible to believe there could be a feeling of distance between me and Tom. The poor image was rendered null and void by our friendship with Lynda, whom we liked and admired so much. We have never spent too much time worrying about the future and, since we already had one child with a handicap and neither John nor I are overly ambitious for our offspring (other than that they are happy, stay true to themselves and feel fulfilled), those hearing expectations were not really a problem. I know one is advised to 'grieve for the child you have lost' and 'learn to love the child you have', but all our tears had been shed during the illness and the child we had left was so unbelievably precious we needed no lessons in loving him. Every day was a day for rejoicing.

Help at Hand

We did need help, though. And that help came in December in the form of John Hurd, then Senior Advisory Teacher (Audiology). The way he threw himself on the floor and played with the nine-month-old Thomas, who was still unable to sit up without a barrage of cushions, endeared him to me immediately. I was convinced he must have young children of his own but found, to my surprise, that I was wrong. Ignorant and vulnerable as I was, it says much for John's approach that he never made me feel inadequate, just inspired. Aware of him ignoring the abundance of inherited toys around, I once watched, fascinated, as he picked up an empty tissue box and he and Tom played endlessly putting a ball of crumpled paper in and out of it and, of course, talking, talking, talking all the time. Words and actions going together, to and fro, making sense to the young child on the floor.

At that stage, lost in admiration for John's skills, I had no real idea of what was expected of me or of Thomas. It took a while to realise that the sessions were for my benefit as much as Tom's, that I was meant to be learning how to play and talk to him. On one early visit the two of them were getting on so well I felt positively superfluous and wondered if I should busy myself elsewhere instead. I loved the way John would tuck Tom under his arm and wander round the room with him, scrutinising the books on the dusty shelves and having earnest 'conversations' about the

With John Hurd on one of his peripatetic visits

French Revolution or whatever title happened to be at eye level. It was all so effortlessly natural, with no pressure on us to *perform*.

John Hurd was far too polite to bully us about the lack of things happening with regard to a hearing aid, and far too professional to tell me in so many words not to put too much faith in local services. He was mystified by the referral to Queen Square, where the consultant had not been expecting such a young baby and had been sent no history of the illness or details of the drugs administered during it. Since Thomas co-operated so well some tests had been done there and the hearing loss confirmed, before we were returned to sender since no hearing aid service was in operation. Nevertheless John's relief was apparent when, after much badgering and frustration, we finally got the correct referral to the Nuffield Centre, part of the Royal National Throat, Nose and Ear Hospital in London.

The appointment was for 26 February 1981. We were seen by a consultant, who asked lots of questions and was fascinated by the way Tom sat at my feet, solemnly turning the pages of a Dick Bruna 'Miffy' book I'd taken with us. He said he'd never seen a child so young handle a book with such interest and care. Enraged at the delay we had experienced in getting a

Not hearing but feeling the sound – Christmas
1981

referral to him for a hearing aid, he pulled out all the stops so that, unheard of, we were able to return the following day and pick up the aid and ear-moulds.

So there we were at last. Thomas had his body-worn aid – a daunting thing for a fumble-fisted mother who dreaded its insertion – but he accepted it immediately and wore it for short periods every day to get used to it. Although in turn I totally accepted his deafness, on one early visit to the hospital when I watched a doctor extricate a large plug of wax from Tom's ear, for one brief, glorious and misguided moment I thought to myself, 'There, that's all it was – *wax*. He's not deaf after all!' And then reality returned . . . Tom's profound bi-lateral sensori-neural deafness could not really be denied, even in my wildest dreams.

When we returned to the Nuffield to see a teacher of the deaf (or maybe a speech therapist, I hadn't yet got to grips with the different professionals at that stage) he enthralled Tom with a Fisher Price Jack-in-the-Box toy. I remember him saying Thomas would learn to lip-read and, hopefully, follow commands, even if a hand was covering the speaker's mouth. One thing he said, as he discussed words and the shapes they made on the lips, really caught my imagination. 'Yellow is a lovely word to see'.

'Yellow is a lovely word to *see*'. It opened my mind to the possibility of making learning language fun for Thomas. Suddenly it seemed like an exciting challenge. Around this time, full of this new enthusiasm and information I was to glean from the courses we attended, I wrote an article using this very phrase as my title and beginning with what I felt was a poignant thought. 'Thomas and his grandmother both had hearing aids for their birthdays in March this year – the only difference being that she was eighty-seven and he was only one'. And I must admit he took to his better than she did to hers which, until the day she died, spent much of its time in its box, merrily whistling away.

At that time the Nuffield Centre was offering residential courses for parents at an old house in Ealing, West London. Several families were invited to stay for four days and attend talks and sessions with different specialists (speech therapists, audiologists, teachers) all on a reassuringly informal basis. The consultant put arrangements in hand immediately for us to go in March since, as he explained to his colleague meaningfully, 'She knows already'. Had Tom's deafness been diagnosed for the first time on that February afternoon we would have been given time to digest the news and start to come to terms with it before embarking on such a course. As it was we did, indeed, know and I was more than ready to learn more.

In fact I was avid for information. I had already asked John Hurd for some book titles but I must say I found most, other than the invaluable NDCS (National Deaf Children's Society) booklets, depressing in the extreme. Humour and love seemed sadly lacking in many I read. Instead, I formed a picture of a lonely, deaf child, isolated in the midst of his own family, the daily life of which was in ruins. Twenty-one years on I am happy that there are other books on the market which paint a more positive picture. But at that time even Freddy Bloom's *Our Deaf Children into the 80's* (1978) couldn't dispel many fears and already I fiercely disagreed with her on several points. In particular when she made excuses for the fact that the young deaf child cannot take other people's feelings into account 'because he does not know they have any!'

Surely such consideration should be common to every civilised child, hearing or not, and it is up to the parents or carers to provide the climate for it to flourish. I've always felt consideration for another's feelings and possessions was the most important concept we could pass on to our children. Thomas's school reports have always commented on his 'caring

Tom had to get used to cumbersome hearing
aids and harness

and considerate' attitude towards others and I stick by the indignant
remark – 'what rubbish' – I pencilled in the margin of my copy all those
years ago!

On 12 March 1981 Thomas was one year old, a birthday we discovered,
to our delight, he shared with his teacher. That day which we had feared
Tom may never live to see was a very special one. The only place I wanted
to be for a part of it was in church and fortunately there was a Eucharist to
which I took him and where he received a blessing. Of course I couldn't
help thinking back to the day of his birth and not without huge regret for
what had been taken from him. I even wondered if it was somehow selfish
to be rejoicing that *he* had not been taken from *us*.

More and more I think there is a reason that he was saved. He has
touched people's lives as every special child does. This was brought home
to me a few years after his illness. The church service was over and the
organist played the final music, which just happened to be Pachelbel's
'Canon'. Immediately I was transported back to those post-natal days with
the tiny figure snuggled up beside me listening to that special tape I'd
bought of womb sounds, lullabies and other soothing classical music. I
found it impossible not to shed a tear or two. But, blinking them away as I

reached the door, I was stopped by the leader of Junior Church who said they wanted to give their collection money for that term to local deaf children and would I ask the Head of the Hearing Impairment Unit to phone him. Suddenly I felt things had meaning again. Already I found Tom's presence was being felt, making people more aware of deaf children. I feel it is up to us as parents to be open about the problem. To explain the hearing aid, especially to other children, not of course to ask for favours or make unnecessary allowances, but to say 'Here is a deaf child, perfectly normal in every other way; don't be afraid of him. Talk to him. Include him'.

Eye-opening Courses

The days on the Nuffield course at Ealing were an eye-opener. Not only did I learn about decibels, kilohertz, audiograms, strategies for getting and keeping the child's attention ('Did I really need these?', I would ask myself, since Tom never missed a thing, so determined was he to be fully *au fait* with what went on his world) but also the attitudes of other parents. Some found it very daunting, and I must admit it is unnerving to be studied playing with your own child, but it's easier for an expert then to suggest ways of turning games or stories to the best advantage. The sessions helped take away the mystique of all the things that were so new to us.

It was interesting to meet other parents of course. I could empathise with them but I didn't always understand them! The mother of a deaf baby already agonising over the fact that her daughter may grow up to marry a deaf man and they will be labelled 'that deaf couple'. The mother who didn't 'believe' in signing but forced her tense little girl to learn and say the word for 'apple' not because she liked apples but because she'd *got* to learn to say it. The mother who, when asked what she would look for in a school for her deaf child, replied with stars in her eyes, 'One with lots of audiology equipment'. And another who bitterly resented her child's Phonic Ear radio aid because it implied a physical barrier between them. I know we are all different and every family has different priorities and attitudes but how I used to bless John Hurd's good, down-to-earth advice and the way he never held out false hopes and even sometimes positively dashed my naïve enthusiasm for some new development.

In that first of several visits to Ealing I realised speech must be meaningful to the child but by the end of the week I also told myself firmly that I must not lose sight of the fact that, in our case, we were talking about a baby and I resolved not to get too hung up about the odd spontaneous nonsense remark I might make. In fact, when I said something quite babyish to Tom in our bedroom I recall thinking, 'Help! Maybe the room is bugged and I'll be thrown off the course'.

Back home the disturbed behaviour and bad sleep patterns I had been led to expect did not materialise. Tom didn't turn into a disagreeable little stranger overnight and we continued to rejoice in him. If I have a message here for any new parent it is this. If you have the capacity to understand your child, revel in it. Don't ever pretend you cannot understand just for the dubious pleasure of hearing a word stressfully produced from him or her. Where does the satisfaction lie in that? What is so wonderful about the spoken word in those early days?

Years later Tom's uncle suffered a stroke and lost much of his speech overnight. When my sister-in-law told me that speech therapists, seeking to help him regain some, had suggested she pretend she did not understand him and should maybe not accede to his requests until he had formed the word, my blood ran cold. I had heard of this 'method' being used with deaf children in some areas and it really horrified me. If someone suffering the isolation of a stroke or deafness cannot rely on their nearest and dearest to provide understanding in an hour of need what hope is there for any of us? Can it *really* be right to alienate a deaf child or a stricken partner from those on whom they should be able to depend for understanding and support? My letter on these lines to the RNID (Royal National Institute for Deaf People) magazine was published and through it I struck up a postal friendship with a deaf friend in Sheffield – Dorothy Dowling – of whom more later.

As casually as the staff nurse had mentioned deafness that day in hospital, in May 1981 John Hurd brought the conversation round to signing. Had we ever thought about it? What did we know of it?

I had to cast my mind back to my early twenties and to a young couple my friend Barbara and I used to see on the train some evenings. She can no longer remember them but at the time we were fascinated by the way they communicated in sign. They were, we decided, having us on. There couldn't be anything wrong with them. They couldn't be *deaf!* They looked so *normal!* Such is the stuff of ignorance and prejudice . . .

With the warning that we would meet a lot of opposition, John left us to think about the implications of signing, before we embarked on another chapter in our lives . . .

Chapter 3

Take My Hands and Let Them Move

> I never cared about the sounds
> Of radios or bands
> What hurts me is I never heard
> My parent's signing hands.
> (Stephen J. Bellitz, 1983)

'Words are not enough' may seem a strange slogan from a one-time journalist but, especially when applied to a deaf child, they are apt. Words are not enough initially, when there is a whole world to explore and names need to be given to things. Total communication is what counts and that communication needs to come in a format that is appropriate for the situation. Facial expression, eye contact, body language, gesture, lip patterns, signs and voice (and, later, writing) all have a vital part to play. The past two decades have convinced me of that, but when the idea of *signing* was first mooted I admit to wavering after my initial acceptance.

Signing has implications which make it an emotive subject, rather on a par with religion and politics! The arguments against it, from the aural / oral lobby, are based on the assumption that if a deaf child has access to the 'easy' option of signing then he or she will never bother to try and use his or her own voice, or even to lip-read successfully. This viewpoint can be put across very forcefully and I personally find it alarming that so much depends on the area in which one lives and the people with whom one comes into contact in that desperately vulnerable early stage following diagnosis. Families can be influenced in what I now realise is one of the most important decisions they will ever have to make and one that will have repercussions on the remainder of the child's, and possibly their own, life.

But we were so lucky. Our visiting teacher, whom I had already come to see as a trusted friend, constructive in his advice, had explained his viewpoint. Along with so many others he'd graduated from Manchester University convinced that signing was not to be considered as an option. It was a day working with a class of bright young deaf boys who had had a productive morning of menu planning and supermarket shopping, of preparing and cooking a meal for themselves and their teachers that made him re-think. Despite their obvious enthusiasm for the project, when it came to putting their novel experience on to paper they handed him a jumble of words and ideas which had been left to his goodwill to unscramble and make meaningful. Oralism had not led to literacy for them. That reported scenario alone made me think seriously about the logic of signing as a means to language, especially since reading and writing are such huge pleasures to me.

John Hurd had gone on to explain that he'd seen small deaf children wanting something. Pointing, maybe unsuccessfully, getting more and more worked up until in the end both distracted mother and child are in such a state that the frenzied youngster has long since forgotten the object of his desire. As a very laid-back Libran, who'd do anything for a quiet life (no pun intended) I didn't relish the thought of confrontations such as this countless times a day. But on a deeper level I knew I wanted to communicate with this little boy and that if signs would help I wanted to learn. I felt sure John Hurd would not have suggested signing had he not felt Tom's hearing loss was so great that he would need such support (indeed, I knew he felt strongly that some deaf children definitely need not and *should* not sign). Although after our first visit to the Nuffield course in May (thanks to my catching mumps the March one had been aborted) I had a few second thoughts I realised very soon, without a shadow of doubt, that to sign was the best decision I had ever made.

On the residential week at the Nuffield there had been a discussion group on communication methods. Mindful of John's warning I confessed, 'I am going to learn to sign. Do you want me to leave now?' The staff laughed and refuted the very idea – but they did add 'Why not wait a year or two and see how Thomas gets on first?'

With the benefit of hindsight I realise just what precious time we would have wasted if we'd followed this suggestion. All that special pre-nursery time that one can never have again. There are no second chances. Hearing children have language surrounding them and most pick it up effortlessly, subconsciously, incidentally, appearing to ignore what is not relevant to them at that time but somehow, in some amazing way, storing it up for the future.

The deaf baby and toddler, denied this ability to pick and choose aurally, still need to know that people and things have names and that they can make choices – 'orange juice or milk', 'swings or slide', 'blue or green T-shirt'. A toddler's day is full of new discoveries, exciting happenings, sometimes puzzling events. If there is no one with whom to share these experiences, what a sad state of affairs for all concerned.

For our son signs were to be a lifeline into the world. A couple of years later when we returned for our final Nuffield course, their enthusiastic speech therapist admitted to me 'I'm so glad you used signs with Thomas'. She could see that for him it had been right since, despite his poor audiogram, he was doing 'remarkably well'. He was happy, good at communicating and not frustrated. Because, for Thomas, signs led to words and words led to understanding and language that I still find amazing.

It was pointed out to us once, by a teacher in the primary school, that 'mere articulation of sounds is not thought. It follows thought. The teacher using signs can accelerate the child's understanding. When the child no longer needs the tool (of sign language) it can put it away'. A much respected speech therapist at the same meeting considered that if the emphasis on speech is taken off and only sign vocabulary and language are used, then all stress goes so that speech is given a chance to develop normally. It had been her experience that 'the flowing movements of sign seem to assist the speech patterns'.

In Marc Marschark's book *Raising and Educating a Deaf Child* he writes

> Delaying the learning of Sign Language in the hope of developing better speaking skills in deaf children simply does not work in most cases. In fact such delays can make matters more difficult for both children and their parents. The first years of life are when basic language skills develop, and the first two or three years are generally recognised as a critical period for language learning.

As a Director of the Center for Research, Teaching and Learning at the National Technical Institute for the Deaf, College of Rochester Institute of Technology, USA. he writes with a wealth of experience and understanding.

Many people are dismissive about the use of sign. The most unforgivable description is that it is 'dirty'. I am not sure what they mean by this insult. That it's not pure, that it's lazy, that it's rude? Whatever the detractor's problem it's a word I resent most strongly in this context. To see Thomas at one year old sitting up in his pram, gleefully signing 'dog' to me, then looking bewildered because his woolly red mittens cramped his signing style, was anything but dirty. It was enchanting! And it led to a two-way dialogue once he'd drawn my attention to the dog that I hadn't spotted behind me. Already I was acquiring the verbal diarrhoea that means no opportunity for communicating is wasted and it was frustrating when he outgrew the big pram and I found it impossible to find a parent-facing buggy so that we could remain face-to-face on our frequent walks.

Early Signs

'What', John asked me at the outset of signing, 'is the word you need most?' It didn't take long to come up with 'no', feeling very negative as I said it. But it was true since, as a baby starts to walk and explore, it's very often an overworked word in the family, not for any oppressive reason but simply for safety. There were others, of course – 'yes', 'biscuit', 'orange', 'fish', 'cat', 'dog', 'apple', 'car', 'mummy', 'daddy'. And we found them all in the parents' manual with which John presented me. It resembled a giant knitting pattern, unfathomable to the uninitiated, horribly daunting at first – but it was to become my bible.

The signs then in use at the Hearing Impairment Unit to which Tom would be going at the age of three were Paget Gorman Signed Speech (PGSS). The system, in which signs are used to represent each spoken word and the grammar of English, had the advantage of being available in written form and based on 37 basic signs which made it what I have heard described as 'a flawless mirror of the English language and perfect foundation blocks on which to build that language'. On the other hand, it has the disadvantage of having been devised by hearing people and, as such, of not being recognised or used within the Deaf community.

John offered to give me and some local friends a few lessons during his early visits and, rather than copy him, insisted we look up each word in the manual and work out for ourselves, from the detailed and sometimes complicated instructions, exactly how to get all our fingers and thumbs in the right position. The beauty of the signs, once we'd mastered them, was that, because of the concepts, Tom could see that the liquid in the bath, in the beaker, in the pond, in the puddle was all called 'water'. Animals were all based around one hand shape so he could quickly see the difference between cat, dog, bull, cow, rhinoceros, camel, horse, elephant. I always maintain this gave him a head start since I've read of hearing children being told something black and fluffy is a cat and thereafter, for a while, everything resembling that, even grandma's fur hat, is referred to as a cat. Tom suffered no such confusion.

In retrospect, I realise PGSS gave Tom a *sign vocabulary* with which to access English, rather than a *sign language*, but the concepts of colour, animals, time, positions, for example, were so clearly identifiable with their related signs and made such sense to him that I shall always treasure his early exposure to it. Possibly it was far too prescriptive in some ways, and certainly many of the later, lunchtime sessions in the unit, when teachers and parents agonised for what seemed like hours over the pedantic angling of a digit, could have been put to better use in more expressive signing, but as a sure foundation for English it could not have been bettered at that stage

Universal sign for 'good' is applied to mum's
croissants in summer 1983

in Tom's development. In 1985/6 the HIU was to switch to Signed English
which is based on the signs of BSL (British Sign Language) but with English
word order and grammar.

Although PGSS was used in Bromley units it was not taught locally and
my close and very supportive friend, Wendy Atkinson, and I had to attend
classes in the adjacent borough of Croydon, where it was taught in evening
classes but not used in schools! I had not expected to enjoy the sessions at
the end of a busy day with an energetic 18-month-old but they were
tremendous fun and the people learning so interesting themselves. I was
the only parent of a child needing signs; the others were volunteers with
handicapped children, would-be speech therapists, nannies or nurses. We
learnt to sign songs, 'Colours of the Rainbow' being a firm favourite, but
the exam was hard going. How many other exams are there where you're
only allowed to make two mistakes? But we passed and have our certifi-
cates to prove it!

Thomas's confidence grew and grew. The family picked up the signs
and he could express himself and play his rightful part in our everyday life
instead of being marginalised, cut off from us by his deafness as I'd once

Give me 5! Tom signs his order for the
strawberries – summer 1983

been led to believe by the books I'd read. He would scrutinise the contents
of his potty, as toddlers are wont to do, laugh and sign 'fish' or 'snake', refer
to a half-eaten cream cracker on his plate as a 'house', its triangular shape
reminding him of a roof, and so prove to us that his imagination wasn't
stunted by his deafness. He could also interact with others. I can still see
him at 18 months, leaning across from his high chair to warn a seven-year-
old school friend of Daniel's that the apple crumble was 'hot!' That boy
went home a few hours later sufficiently fascinated by Tom to learn some
signs, his favourite being the almost universal one for 'good'.

We revelled in Tom, who had a tremendous sense of fun. It was not long
before his lively imagination gave rein to lions in the kitchen, rendering it
unsafe for him to venture out there alone and, several years later, to a
dramatic, straight-faced saga of a friend's roof being blown off in the gales
and the ensuing damage to the bedrooms. It was not until I phoned up
offering spare duvets that I discovered, to my embarrassment, it was that
vivid imagination at work again.

By the age of two years he had 36 signs (a hearing baby has about 50
words at this age I believe) and six months later had added another 50. He
could say 'please', 'thank you', 'sorry', even 'very sorry' if misdemeanour

warranted it. He could inject expression into his signing; a limp-wristed sign for a boring old glass of water but a really grandiose gesture for a welcome mug of his favourite orange juice. He would refer smugly to himself as a 'good boy', his brothers as 'bad boys', and say 'silly me' if he'd done something stupid. He could eventually take on abstract ideas. On his first morning at Junior Church, where thanks to Father Jeremy's foresight, he was lucky enough to have a leader who happened to be a teacher of the deaf, he came home and announced solemnly that 'God made the world' followed by a very thoughtful, 'and God made the Thomas'. And on the first hot night of summer, when he was looking forward to wearing the new shorts all ready on his chair for the morning, he said and signed his usual 'God bless Mummy and Daddy, Matthew and Daniel' and then lay back with a happy sigh and added 'and God bless little trousers!' Later on he could use words manipulatively, too. He admired my new hair cut when he got in from school but hours later, when I'd refused him something, he retaliated with 'and I *not* like your hair!'

With signs one could reason with him, explain things, include him. He in turn could tell us if he was happy or sad, cold or tired, hungry or thirsty, hurt or cross. And, because we all need an internal language to make plans, order our thoughts, Tom could pass on his own ideas and thoughts, hopes or expectations. He learned what 'wait' meant and astutely summed up a visit to the dentist or clinic as a 'big wait'. By counting the number of bedtimes before an event he could understand something of the passage of time, and contain his impatience a little. He could also engage in dialogue to negotiate. For example, aged three, when told at the swimming pool that it was time to come out of the water, he pleaded 'One more! Me frog. Me fish. Me finished!' then dutifully did as he'd been asked.

As a parent it's always a salutary lesson to discover that one's offspring are brighter than oneself. I wasn't prepared to have that sobering realisation dawn when Tom was only three but it was a lesson I had to learn early. We had returned from some days on the Nuffield course and I was putting the washing on the line, when the wind blew the front door shut behind me. Tom was still in the house and Grannie was upstairs and, like him, oblivious to the sound of the doorbell. What to do? I managed to attract Tom's attention through the window and sign to him to fetch my shoulder bag. I was planning to ask him to post me a pen and paper from it so that I could write a note which Tom could take upstairs to my mother, asking her to come down and open the door for me. (Tom himself was too small to turn the lower door knob and upper lock which needed to be done simultaneously.) Just how complicated could one get? Tom, so sensibly, simply passed the key from my bag out through the letter box into my shaking hands. *I* was the one who felt small then . . .

Power of Language

Hearing infants use language to predict and anticipate events, to report on happenings, to project themselves into imaginary experiences. With some deaf children and adults it seems that all too often a lack of language, signed or spoken, means they can rarely move beyond the concrete, simple, here-and-now experience and, as such, abstract ideas are all too often beyond them. With this in mind, I turned to a favourite writer, Leila Berg, whose book *Reading and Loving* had been an earlier inspiration, and found she had this to say about language acquisition:

> Babies learn from birth to talk. They do it of their own accord. They don't have to go to school first, to learn phonetics or sentence structure. They learn in the cradle and the pram – first from their own free playful exploration, then from the important people round them, their own important people.
>
> And if the child's 'important people' encourage and delight in the child, and if neither they nor society clamps down, then the child not only becomes fluent, but learns the self-organising power of words . . . the power that enables a child to predict and plan a future.

Substitute the word 'sign' for 'talk' and I think, in our case, we had a recipe for what I now regard as success.

Because communication was established so early and so successfully, I can honestly say that we had no temper tantrums from Tom, other than very minor ones common to any two-year-old when temporarily thwarted. He was just over four before he said the first thing I couldn't understand. It was some hours later, long after he'd gone to bed in disgust, that I fathomed it out, 'Mim Barra' – of course, Mrs Barrett, the new special support assistant at the unit! I was so relieved I wanted to wake him up and redeem myself but that seemed selfish so instead I stayed downstairs feeling really shaken. Of course in this instance there was no sign so I needn't have felt guilty but, without access to signing, that dreadful sense of inadequacy and impotence would have been with me permanently I feel sure. And there are other sound reasons for signing. Thanks to brain-scanning techniques, neurologists have discovered that it uses the same left hemisphere of the brain that is used in processing spoken language, and that makes sound sense to me.

At a study day I attended a mother stood up and confessed that she had finally *had* to learn to sign, *in desperation*, when her child was three. I think by starting, not in desperation but willingly, when Tom was a baby, we prevented all the frustration and misunderstanding that can build up on both sides. I wanted to open the doors of communication between us, not shut them only to have to fling them open in despair when all else had failed. So many missed opportunities, so many heartaches, so much frustration and hurt could have resulted. And, because we always used our voices as we signed, Tom lip-read well from an early age and now, although his own speech is not very intelligible to naïve listeners, he uses excellent lip patterns himself which can aid their understanding. I was horrified when I heard of a deaf teenager who had been brought up orally. She learnt to sign eventually and her mother decided to learn too, only to have the daughter round on her with the words, 'I talk with you. I only use signs with my deaf friends'. Hidden in that statement I think there must lie a sad history of hurt.

Some deaf adults we meet appear to envy Tom the easy communication we share; others are amazed that I, being hearing, can sign! Some of Tom's old school friends with more hearing have dropped the use of sign, no longer needing it personally but, of course, employ it with him. Other friends, with excellent speech and some useful hearing, prefer to identify themselves with the Deaf community and now revel in the use of British Sign Language despite an oral education and upbringing.

To my mind, signing is a skill which should be widely taught to hearing people; its uses are endless. Judging by the over-subscribed sign language classes, mostly taught by deaf people, who are the ideal tutors, there is a huge interest in the subject now, together with a whole array of books, CD Roms and videos to consolidate the classes. And with the advent of the book *Baby Signs* by Linda Acredolo and Susan Goodwyn (1996) even parents of hearing babies are being encouraged to 'Talk to your baby before your baby can talk'. And I'm all for it since it comes naturally to me when I'm interacting with a small baby who can't yet speak. These two authors maintain that sign language 'speeds up the process of learning to talk, stimulates intellectual development, enhances self-esteem and strengthens the bond between parent and infant'. If it can do that for a hearing infant, just think what it can do for a deaf one.

Signing has an application for the rest of the family, too. Countless times in situations where distance, solemnity or noise separates us we've blessed the ability to be able to communicate silently. (I didn't even resent the fact that my husband could sign 'silly moo' to me from the bottom of the garden when I was washing up by the kitchen window.) Younger siblings seem to pick up the signs naturally and older ones enjoy the challenge of acquiring a new skill. Daniel's enthusiasm and proficiency took shape simultaneously with a craze for break-dancing and we reprimanded him one supper-time for indulging in the hand movements of the latter at the table. His indignant retort – 'I wasn't break-dancing I was only asking for the cheese in sign' put us to shame!

Educational Observations

Before Tom started in the nursery school John visited us once a week. I think he was as delighted as I was (although his bluff exterior would always belie it) when Tom put together his first sentence at the age of 18 months. 'You' (pointing to John) 'go' (pointing to the door) 'bye-bye' (waving) 'broom-broom' (vocalising and miming turning the steering wheel of the unseen van he knew was parked outside). Point was taken; lesson was over. Exit John Hurd!

Thomas would organise games around the room, working ideas out for himself and John would look at him, shake his head in disbelief and reflect quietly 'but deaf children don't play games like this . . . '. Maybe not if they are unsure of themselves, uncertain of their role, overcome by an inability to communicate with their carers and siblings, have no conception of turn-taking, are oblivious to the days of the week, when or why things happen. It's *communication* that builds confidence. One deaf friend recalls often being bundled into a car and driven off with her parents, never certain whether the destination was going to be school, seaside, shops or whatever. Is it any wonder deaf children can so easily become confused, frustrated, aggressive or withdrawn?

A confident Tom joins in the Conga led by Wendy Atkinson who made music fun for him

Amidst the deluge of information and advice that is offered initially one can be in danger of losing the one thing that matters most at this stage – childhood itself. Those precious early years are for having fun, for enjoyment, for doing deliciously silly things that can never be recaptured in later years. And if those formative years are spent confronting the child in a learning situation devoid of humour, as can so easily be the temptation when you are suddenly overwhelmed with the enormity of the task before you, you have lost something more precious than you imagine. For the sake of a few words produced under stress you have sacrificed too much. I still remember feeling affronted when the grandmother of a non-signing deaf child bore down on us in the supermarket one day to enquire how Tom's 'conditioning' was going. I felt physically sick that such a word could be applied to my one-year-old and I still believe that for him the oral/aural only route would have led to little language and no clear speech, a fate I find too frightening to contemplate.

When Tom started nursery school at the age of three years the signs stood him in good stead. He arrived there with words and phrases he would need. The Head of the Unit was delighted. When he felt ill during his second day there, he could tell her. She recalls that on one occasion when they had been learning about 'real and pretend' using genuine milk versus white flour and water solution, getting the children to smell and taste the difference, he cottoned on to the concept and shortly afterwards went to the Wendy house and lay down on the bed declaring 'I'm *pretending* to be ill'. The ability to take a new word and play with it and use it again in an equally correct but quite different context has amazed and delighted teachers and parents alike. The idea of a gravy *boat* amused him hugely! Happily, even in his twenties the delight in the vagaries of the English language continues.

I am well aware that it is not English but British Sign Language (BSL) with its own grammar, syntax and vocabulary, that is regarded as the natural language of deaf people. Without doubt it is a beautiful, visual language. But unless the child is one of the 10% born into a Deaf family where the language is genuinely handed down from generation to generation I don't really see how it is any more 'natural' than Signed English or Sign Supported English. For Thomas the near tragedy that overtook him at five months did not automatically deny him access to our family and culture overnight and qualify him instead solely for the Deaf world. Meningitis removed his ability to hear but it didn't remove him from his family and their community.

Years ago, a reader's letter in a woman's magazine caught my eye, about a young boy describing his baby brother. 'He's got some teeth now', he'd said, 'but his words haven't come in yet!' I shall be everlastingly grateful that I had the chance to let my hands give Tom the words he needed before

Powers of observation in a 3 year old's drawing
of his daddy

his came in. I am acutely conscious of the fact that hearing people who congratulate me on my signing skills, such as they are, have no idea how much better they could and should be and that I shall be learning for the rest of my life to try and improve. I am also painfully aware that when deaf people are amazed that a hearing mother signs with a deaf child it speaks volumes for their own upbringing, when no doubt a teacher of the deaf or other professional told their parents never to sign. I am aware that the relationship I share with Tom is especially blessed because of it. I see the hand of God in this, because He sent a man whose name was John . . .

Just think how much we take *spoken* language for granted! We expect our hearing children to acquire it automatically and, if we are honest, we can remember very little later of their efforts to do so. 'Motherese' is acknowledged as legitimate, modified early communication, even though meaningless 'baby talk' is now frowned upon, and every family treasures the sayings of its young – the mispronounced words, the coined phrases, the garbled grammar. Toddler Daniel's 'leaving lorry' was applauded as an excellent description of a removal van, especially since we had been all too aware that Matthew, our eldest, had delayed speech. With him, when I queried the fact that he used only 20 words at the age of two years I was reprimanded by the health visitor for being 'technical'! A year later, after Matthew had a febrile convulsion following a fever, our GP found his speech 'appalling' and referred him to a speech therapist. She incurred my wrath by despairing that 'all he wants to do is *talk*' when he had some really exciting news to impart after his grannie had been taken, with a burst appendix, to hospital by ambulance!

With a deaf child one can't help treasuring every manifestation of language in whatever form it takes. I have a collection of scribbled utterances or signs hastily consigned to the backs of envelopes for future reference (i.e. this book)! 'Chasing' language, by whatever route, meant that everything Tom signed or attempted to say became a bonus. Into the family folklore went 'Father Crippers' in the run up to his third Christmas and what could be more endearing than a marsupial 'Mama-roo'? When I discovered that Tom knew our postman's name was Bob my joy knew no bounds. Why? Because *I* had never told him that; he'd somehow picked it up!

Tom especially enjoyed teasing me about my shortcomings, in particular my inability to drive. Drawing friend Wendy's car one day he said to me 'You *must* drive a car'. I explained, 'I don't know how'. Tom insisted, 'You must drive Wendy's car'. I demurred, 'Policeman will put me in prison because I don't know how to drive a car'. Tom retaliated, 'Wendy is clever. You sit on Wendy's lap and drive. Yes, yes, yes'. Absent-mindedly I signed 'yes' by mistake. Tom, delighted, chortled 'Ha, ha. You said "yes"'. Then, turning to his brother for confirmation of my *faux pas*: 'Dan, you saw! Mummy said "yes"!'

I don't remember envying my friends and their hearing children, or not often anyway, but I do recall one occasion when Daniel was fascinated by a friend's one-year-old whose first words happened to be 'teddy bear'. He asked little Andrew to repeat them, over and over again, and I found it strange that an eight-year-old schoolboy should be so enchanted with the sound. And then it dawned on me just what he'd missed with his own baby brother and that he had made his request for the sheer joy of hearing 'normal' words from a hearing child.

Beginning with Books

Our peripatetic teacher, John, knew how much Tom and I enjoyed sharing books. 'But how do you read to him?' he enquired one day. I guessed the 'correct' answer would be 'sitting opposite him so that he can see my face and hands'. But it would not have been true. Like any child of that age, he sat on my lap and we enjoyed the closeness the activity brings, a closeness so beautifully brought out in Leila Berg's captivating book *Reading and Loving*. After I had heard her enthralling talk at a National Childbirth Trust meeting locally, I had bought a copy when Daniel was a toddler. Re-reading it after Tom was deafened I found her wise words held a particular poignancy since they focused on sharing language and were still relevant, even for a baby with a hearing impairment.

In this new millennium I'd love to see her book used as the antidote to the trend for pushing infants headfirst into the technological age of computers, where the only mouse is certainly not a toy one and the only lap has the word 'top' after it! The tactile joy of handling a book and sharing a story with an important adult is something that I would hate to think was denied to a tiny child, deaf or hearing. Tom was astute enough to know he needed to keep turning round to me to see what I was saying but the shared, close experience was more important to us both than any amount of face-to-face 'learning'. And I should have known better than to think John would criticise our reading style; that was just one more instance when I found we were on the same wavelength. As he said 'there's a lot more than just reading going on' when you share a book in this way. I think this must be what Leila Berg herself calls 'the emotional feel of communication'.

In the mid-1980s a working party was set up to consider changing from Paget Gorman to Signed English in order that our deaf children would eventually acquire BSL for relaxation within the Deaf community, etc. I had mixed feelings and admitted at the time that I felt as if we had been given a lovely present (PGSS) that had been taken away from us before we'd finished using it, but I was proved wrong. The changeover was simple, it seemed, because we already had signing skills. Teachers, parents and children alike made the switch quite painlessly and, much as I loved them at the time, I have now forgotten most of the Paget Gorman signs.

Of course all parents feel they should have the right to choose the early mode of communication for their child. (To be honest, if Thomas had been our first child and I had been very young and self-conscious I doubt I should have opted so easily for something that calls attention to a condition many would prefer to ignore.) But it should be an *informed* choice. I know that without the benefit of signing much of the minutiae of daily life would have been denied to Tom. If he had to rely on lip-reading for every little inconsequential remark, observation, joke, exclamation, fleeting idea I wanted to share, I would never have inflicted them on him. The concentration required in lip-reading is exhausting and I would have felt it unfair to expect him to use it other than for intensely meaningful rather than mundane matters. But is that what life should be like?

To me it feels right that signing should be available to all deaf children like a key. It can unlock the door to communication, make sense of a silent world, give the child an internal language and a positive identity, an ability to share his thoughts and organise his life. Some children will need this key all their lives. Some will need it now and again, and others will throw it away when they no longer require it. But without it, the door that never opens can confine the child to a prison through no fault of his own.

On an all too rare visit after Tom started school John Hurd watched him argue with me one day. 'Just think' he said, with a wry smile, 'you could have saved yourself all this if only you'd never learnt to sign!'

Chapter 4

Channels of Communication

I do actually believe that the desire to communicate is almost on the same level as the primal human drives for food, sex, and possibly aggression. (David Attenborough, *Good Housekeeping*)

It was a sad occasion when John Hurd paid his last visit to us as Tom's peripatetic teacher. It felt like the end of an era and even friend Wendy's small daughter realised the implications. 'Does that mean the sign language van won't be calling any more?' (John drove a small white van from his home in West Sussex to his job in Bromley each day.)

The only Hearing Impairment Units in the London Borough of Bromley are part of the Darrick Wood Schools in Orpington, situated just behind Farnborough Hospital, facing Tugmutton Common. During Tom's illness my husband and I had managed to have half an hour away from the ward, once the future seemed more certain, and we had parked by the common to share a sandwich. It seemed ironic that we should have done so now that Thomas was about to start in the nursery there, several miles away from our home, at the tender age of three.

Because I have never summoned up the courage to learn to drive Tom had to do three full days a week, in order to travel on the school bus provided. That seemed preferable to catching four buses a day to get there and back. Naturally I had qualms but such was my confidence in the unit itself and in Tom's own confidence and ability to cope and express himself that I didn't feel too uneasy, just disappointed that our precious time together should be so curtailed.

We took him in ourselves for the first few days, of course, in order that his experience of the school bus was on the homeward journey with me waiting at the other end. Despite an escort who, in my opinion, bore more than a passing resemblance to cartoonist Giles's forbidding Gran, Tom couldn't wait to get on the bus and the signed and spoken 'boo buth' rang through the house for weeks on end! No doubt the fact that his elder brother had always had to go to school in this fashion made it socially acceptable to him but I had cause to be particularly grateful for Tom's 'boo buth' some years later when I saw the original stage version of the award-winning play 'Gary' by Roy Winston, starring our friends Sarah Scott and Ray Harrison Graham. In the opening scene deaf Gary, who was made to sit on his hands in time-honoured fashion at school, is heard tortuously enunciating 'blue bus' as he plays with his toys, whereupon his hitherto anguished parents gleefully label him 'oral' and the pattern for his future is set. As Ray's fabulous narrative rap went: 'Gary had learned to crawl and walk, surely he could learn to talk'. How comforting it was to sit in the theatre, remembering, and knowing that Tom's utterance was born of joy and delight in his mode of transport, not wrung painfully and inappropriately from him! Again, without John Hurd's input I think I might well have been squirming in my seat at the Arts Theatre as the tragedy of Gary's life without signs unfolded on the stage.

Of all the many good ideas I gleaned from the Ealing courses, the one that was most fun to put into practice was the photographic scrapbook. Of course every family hoards its snapshots, and they usually find their way into an album sooner or later, but with a deaf child the photographic record has so much more to offer. We photographed everyday events (bath time, washing up, posting letters) and special occasions (birthday parties, train rides, church events) and in no time at all the scrapbooks with their simple captions became lovely, personalised reading books which Tom would turn to again and again. They were also useful to take to friends or relatives or to his first playgroup, to break the ice, to open up channels of communication and provide a talking point, as well as to remind him of people we might be visiting, or events that were about to happen again.

The first volume started on his second birthday and shows him swimming in the baby pool at Crystal Palace, meeting Dan from school, looking at books with his teacher, waiting patiently in his high chair for supper, having a bath, using his speech trainer, visiting cousins and paternal grandmother, welcoming a new rabbit and showing an old friend of mine the sign for it. He's seen blowing bubbles, dandelions, candles, picking strawberries, swinging, sliding, feeding the ducks, admiring the new car. All that language, all those talking points for him, all those memories for me! At an avant-garde, interactive play on Bosnia I attended, the audience were asked what they would grab if fleeing their home. I was made to feel stupidly sentimental when I replied without hesitation 'photographs'. 'You can't eat photographs' scorned the interrogating actor. Overcome with embarrassment I had to agree he was right but some years later I felt my answer was vindicated when I talked to a friend whose husband's Jewish family had fled Germany before the war. The photographs they salvaged proved so precious to Joan and Steffen, who could trace the family resemblances in their own daughter and son, long after his parents had departed this life. And in a very moving news story I read of a Kosovan father finally reunited with his family by following a trail of torn photographs his wife had strewn as a clue to their escape route. Sometimes food is not the most important thing, after all. *Our* photographs hardly merit a mention in the same paragraph as such momentous events but, in their own way, they were a lifeline and are now a source of joy and remembrance to us, too.

Nearly every experience is worthy of recording, no matter how mundane it may seem since that's exactly what you need to capture for useful, everyday language You don't need to wait till the child is looking cute, clean or even happy – you just need to snap away and record the event for the scrapbook. As other mums have remarked, '*Every* child should have one!' For the deaf youngster whole sequences of events can be recorded. For example, going to choose a Christmas tree, carrying it home, decorating it, sitting amid the presents beneath it, stripping it on Twelfth Night and finally helping plant it in the garden! We have shots of Tom stirring the pudding mixture and then admiring it in all its glossy, black glory on Christmas day, hanging up his empty stocking, and a beatific expression as he prodded its exciting bulges the following day. He was normally quite happy to be caught by my snapping but on rare occasions would pull the sort of face he knew I would not commit to film! Or in third rate movie star style would come over all camera shy and put up a hand to refuse the publicity.

Confidence Building

For the start of school the photographic book was of utmost importance. I photographed him on the common as we made our way for his first pre-school visit and into the book also went the photograph of the Head of Unit, his teacher-to-be, the classroom assistant and, of course, the school bus! He was photographed drinking with a straw, alongside his hearing peers and their teacher. All this was good for reminding, discussing and confidence-building before the start of the summer term and his advent into the nursery.

When the time came we used the instant camera purchased with our first Attendance Allowance (now the Disability Living Allowance) for photographs of Tom and me preparing his lunch-box and carefully engineered a photo opportunity with the positioning of a friend at the front gate to record the hopefully happy moment of his first homecoming and thereby reinforce the fact that I would always be there waiting for him after school. We were even lucky enough to find a school-bag with a bus motif and the words 'All Aboard' on it to tie in with his mode of transport.

After his first day in the nursery class he proudly bore home a cut-out of a black tadpole, had learnt the sign for it and could also make a good approximation of the sound of the word. A rewarding moment for us all, allied with relief that he'd coped with all the new experiences the day had involved!

During his first week one of the topics was trains and he showed his understanding of the concept of 'tomorrow' by explaining that the next day he would be going on one. The first sign he made when he woke up that morning was 'train' and before long we were boarding one for our trip to the Nuffield Centre. On his return to school he was overjoyed about a request for wellington boots, knowing they heralded exciting happenings!

He continued with his fascination for the blue bus, talking about it with shining eyes and a big grin. The blue bus became the answer for everything. 'What did you do in PE today?' 'Boo buth!' He learnt the days of the week. The invaluable home/school books were the link between us and his teachers and gave me the topics he was currently working on. I made a scrapbook with relevant pictures to go through at home.

In May he started wearing a Phonic Ear radio aid for the first time. Alas, my high hopes for it were unfounded. I remembered the glowing reports I'd heard from a mum at Ealing but it never worked like that for Tom. But there were other compensations. The Unit Head told me everyone was delighted with Tom who would talk to anyone and was so friendly and confident. To me that was a relief since John Hurd had written such a well-observed and sensitive summing-up of Tom before he started in the nursery that I was afraid, in the perverse way of a three-year-old, our son would somehow prove him wrong and behave disgracefully!

I am pleased with Thomas' development, which is largely due to his intelligent, supportive family. This little boy uses some approximations to speech but he communicates with gesture and some Paget Gorman. I am especially delighted by his willingness to communicate experiences (as I arrived for my last visit he 'told' me that he had chased the naughty cat, which had run up a tree). He is a friendly child who expects to be understood. When playing alone he often uses his voice, with a fairly good range of intonations.

Tom has a very good memory for things, people and incidents and he assigns his own gestures to each of these, which he will use consistently. His small signs/names for people suggest minute observations. He also seems to grasp the 'essential quality' of a thing or an animal and will show, in his movement or stance, that he is experiencing something of the essence of the object. I feel that a teacher of dance/drama would be thrilled to see him. He likes to play with trains and cars (mostly in spectacular crashes) but he also likes to play little scenes (e.g. the naughty baby going to bed, the little boy being told off by his mother, who says sorry) but he will insist on reversing the roles with his playmate. He has been encouraged to share, take turns and to 'say' sorry and thank you. (John Hurd, 10.3.1983)

This letter helped soften the blow of the early schooling. It's easy for parents to rejoice in their children and cherish every little aspect of them but to think that someone outside the family could see so much in Thomas was really heart-warming. Watching Tom imagining himself to be a pigeon, strutting and 'pecking' in a puddle on the promenade at Eastbourne, bore out the drama bit for me, as did the time in the bathroom when he was pretending to be a baby. Simply by rolling on to the outside of his feet, to indicate the bulk of an imaginary nappy, he achieved exactly the right effect as he stood there with an innocent expression! And I was always convinced that, should we ever be unfortunate enough to suffer a car crash, we would turn round to find Tom signing 'good' with a huge beam on his face!

The new topic of tadpoles still figured largely in his conversation. He peered into a rather seedy jar of raspberry jam one teatime and said / signed 'tadpoles!' very seriously. And even a month after starting school he was still starry-eyed at the very thought of the blue bus and, when with us, became very excited at the mere sight of roads down which it travelled on what was of necessity a very roundabout route across the borough to school. Although he had to leave early and didn't get home until nearly 5 p.m. he had, fortunately, inherited the family ability to fall asleep anywhere, any time, so often the journey home was an unwinding period for him.

Twenty years on re-reading the 33 home / school books to refresh my memory of his early years was not always the unmitigated delight I'd imagined it would be. There's a lot about woolly hats and wet pants (continually querying the whereabouts of the former and apologising for the latter) and there are also references to his tiredness and short temper at home. But also the ongoing saga: 'What animal at school today?' 'Boo buth!'

There was only one occasion on which his pants were soiled, about which he was very shamefaced. Two days later he bounced in after school and announced that the pants he had on were not his own. Drawing the obvious conclusion and fearing the worst again, my face fell a little, only to perk up immediately as he chortled '*ha, ha!*' and I realised he was just teasing me. Such confidence, not only in his language but in his attitude to life and his relationship with me!

He was three years old before he was issued with his first post-aural hearing aids. Having struggled with two body-worn aids for a couple of years this was a good moment. Those long leads and the harness and the constant searching for dungarees with strategically placed pockets had become a pain although, bless him, he never refused to wear the aids or threw them down the loo or did any of the other dire things I've known deaf children resort to. A neighbour's small daughter still had no idea what they were for. 'Oh look', she'd said one day, 'Tom's got his little camera on'!

Tom insisted on being teacher at home. His giant Galt wall frieze was the cause of much extra-curricular activity. 'Show me your . . . ' he would prompt and I would get a clap or a 'good' sign each time I pointed to the right thing. The adhesive vinyl figures from Early Learning Centre were very useful at this time as he loved all the different, everyday scenes and they were wonderful for language, as were the huge range of delightful and durable Playmobil models.

Wendy had her third daughter that summer of 1983 and Thomas was fascinated by the baby, especially her tiny hands and feet, to which he insisted on drawing everyone's attention. The album shows him standing absolutely transfixed by her – and absolutely terrified by the golden labrador puppy that arrived in her family at much the same time. He did, however, find the latter's name, Muffin, much easier to say than Elizabeth!

When Tom wasn't being a teacher, it seemed he was being a performer. I can see him still, gyrating on the grass, 'singing' loudly into the mike (an old broom handle stuck into the earth) miming a pop concert with his brothers. But fond as he was of them, and wedded as he was to his own scrapbooks, he was very confused and not a little unhappy about our old photo albums. Who were these small children wearing familiar clothes, with *his* daddy, in *his* garden? Some years later we had our old ciné films, warts and all, put on to a video, in sequence. Tom was amused and delighted then by Daniel playing to the camera as he picked blackberries on Chislehurst Common the summer before he himself was born. 'Oh, I *love* that boy' he announced. All was forgiven for having come before him in the pecking order!

Books were a lifeline for explaining things. He was horrified when he saw sheep shearing on the television and was convinced the animal was 'broken'. I had to hunt for a book to show the whole process before he was satisfied no harm was being done. Words and lip patterns amused him. He found it excruciatingly funny that 'camel' looks like 'apple' on the lips. And I was amused to come across him one day hunting for a favourite old pseudo-Roman ring of Dan's to which he'd taken a shine. 'Where my wife, where my wife?' he was muttering to himself, having obviously confused the similar signs, and therefore the words, for ring and wife!

At three and a half, along with his brothers who had both had squints and corrective surgery when they were small, he was checked by the orthoptist at the local children's hospital. Because we were familiar with the eye tests I had made an identical letter chart and gone through the procedure with him beforehand so he would know what to expect and be prepared to co-operate. I wasn't prepared for her reaction to him, however. She read his notes, looked him up and down and announced 'I see, he's deaf and dumb'. I knew even in the so-called enlightened eighties people often expected deaf people to be automatically dumb but I hadn't dreamed I would encounter that sort of outmoded attitude in a medical professional. 'He may be deaf', was my angry retort, 'but he certainly isn't dumb'!

He had already produced his first nine word sentence when his large wooden cot-bed was replaced by an exciting new bouncy divan: 'New bed me. No jumping; fall down, bang head'. By now he was able to ask complicated questions. Was his brother going to hospital in an ambulance or on a 'tall red bus'? Just as the Paget Gorman sign manual was my bible, Usborne's *Thousand First Words* was his. He loved the shapes on the lips of 'buffer' and 'buffalo' and we had endless fun with this book at bedtime.

Tom's third Christmas seemed extra special. The scrapbook records him at his first Christingle service on Christmas Eve, looking wonderingly at the crib, clutching his orange with its red ribbon, dried fruit and candle. The following day he behaved beautifully throughout the long service although towards the end he couldn't help himself saying/signing 'Hurry up!' Just then a mum brought her restless young baby to the back of the church. Tom's face lit up. 'Baby Jesus?' he queried, hopefully.

Over the holiday he was his old, relaxed and amusing self and we have memorable photos of him enjoying every aspect of Christmas. On the last day of December 1983 I recorded with joy that he said and signed 'I love you' to me for the very first time. A really special moment. As in Erma Bombeck's thought-provoking prose 'These mums share special gifts' from *Motherhood – The Second Oldest Profession* (1983) I felt I had been 'blessed with a child less than perfect' and I was indeed one of that number who would 'never take for granted a spoken word'.

Early in 1984 we went to our last Nuffield family week at Ealing. They were delighted with Tom's co-operation and progress and no longer seemed to have any reservations about his use of sign. And, even with sign, it was still often the spoken phrase which enchanted him. 'Label-at-the-back' became a favourite mantra after we'd once employed it when he was dressing. He sorted out the life cycle, too. 'Cows are mummies', he said, 'and bulls are daddies'. Then with a big and knowing grin, 'and baby pigs are me!'

Acquiring New Skills

At the age of four he started swimming lessons in Beckenham, having progressed from the mother and baby pool at Crystal Palace Sports Centre. He got off to a good start and the other pupils were soon being told to watch and copy him. Another new skill was riding the bicycle which he got for his fourth birthday and for which he was anxious to discard the stabilisers as quickly as possible. On Mothering Sunday he collected his bunch of daffodils from the chancel steps, then brought them down and presented them to me with a deep and solemn bow, much to the delight of my fellow worshippers.

Two months after his birthday Tom had mastered his bike without stabilisers, and this from a boy who had been so late walking and whose balance I'd despaired of, convinced he'd totter his way into his teen age! I wasn't allowed to mention brakes, however, since he took it to mean the beloved bike was broken. He could also swim a few strokes without armbands and it wasn't long before he relinquished them altogether and was soon able to swim under water and do the back crawl.

His four-year check with the GP was encouraging. The doctor had taken the trouble to borrow equipment to check her own voice level, a thoughtful touch which I appreciated greatly, and Tom was able to build the bricks and sort and name the colours beautifully. 'Children with specific handicaps are often ahead of their peers in other respects', I was told.

Sometimes it seemed that he reacted to noise. The most surprising was the sound of the bathwater running away, to which he would often turn. It was noisy but, of course, he was wearing no aids in the bath and I often wondered if it was the pull of the water as it drained away that he felt as it coincided with the last, loud gurgle. On one occasion a xylophone was accidentally kicked by one of his brothers and to our surprise Tom pointed to his ears, opened the door and ran into the hall to check the front door. But even if he had heard something how would he know the sound resembled that of a door bell?

Disturbing News for the Nursery

Around this time came the news of the threatened closure of the nursery class, the implications of which for the deaf children were alarming. Despite its size, the London Borough of Bromley had only three nursery classes in total, and Darrick Wood was the only one with deaf children. Even if provision had been continued for that small minority, there is no way we would have allowed him to cross the borough to school if it meant he would have only the company of hearing-impaired peers. We felt the behaviour, language patterns, and so on of hearing children were essential

Tom uses his Phonic Ear radio aid and I wear the microphone as we pose for the *Kentish Times* during our nursery campaign

It made a change for Tom to have a professional wielding the camera!

The *Kentish Times* included his brothers in their
series of photographs during our fight to save
the nursery

to him, all the more so because his long days meant he had little contact
with local friends during the week.

It was to be my first taste of the campaigning which I now realise tends to
become part and parcel of life for any caring parents when there are
offspring with special needs. Support was requested and received from
Farnborough Hospital, the Nuffield Centre, speech therapists and from
our own rector. We lobbied the councillors, wrote to local papers, two of
which ran stories on Tom. Missing the point entirely, one local councillor
called round and was at pains to point out that often parents of 'normal'
children didn't want them to be educated alongside handicapped ones!
(Eventually a more enlightened attitude than his prevailed and we won the
day.)

The fight was very time-consuming and I had had enough when one
day, waving goodbye to the photographer and reporter who had just interviewed us, we took off in the car *en famille* for a day at the seaside. On the
way to Eastbourne we were stuck in slow-moving traffic and travelled for
miles behind a minibus full of deaf adults enthusiastically signing away. I

couldn't believe my eyes! At that point in time all I really wanted to do was to take time out of the whole deaf scene.

Fringe Benefits

But for Tom there were compensations in being deaf. He loved the special police day for special needs children, as can be seen in the photograph we have of him sitting beside Floella Benjamin, beaming broadly and clutching the famous Humpty from the dearly loved 'Play School' television programme. He even had a ride in a police car and saw his brother Matthew there, with his special school. It was one occasion among many when it was poor eight-year-old Daniel who was the one who felt deprived. But I was so proud of his relationship with Tom and his natural proficiency with the signs, and he himself remarked one day that he didn't think we would have had nearly as much fun as a family if Tom had not been deaf!

Some time after John Hurd gave me its details following his first visit, I became a committee member of Bromley Chain, a local charity linking deaf and hearing people, founded (mainly by parents of deaf children) in the year of Tom's birth, oddly enough. In 1984 we entered a float in the Bromley Carnival and great fun was had dressing up the boys and our godchildren's young sister, Sarah, as clown, French onion seller, Worzel Gummidge and Aunt Sally respectively. I was photographed for the scrapbook machining baggy pants and adding patches and braces for

A poignant Bank Holiday sees Tom on the
Bromley Chain carnival float

Tom's clown costume, then practising in the garden applying face paints and giving him a bucket of 'pretend' water! And all the time at the back of my mind was the painfully poignant memory of that other August Bank Holiday that had been such a turning point in our lives.

Whatever had been collected during the summer holiday went straight into a new school bag 'to show Mrs W' Tom's teacher who had not been far from his thoughts for the duration. A very encouraging sign! Thomas, it seemed from the home/school book at the start of the new term, was slightly shy about assuming the role of teacher at school. Dan and I had to smile at this piece of news, since at home he would give it his all and line us up to ask us names of things – 'How many?' – 'Show me the . . . '. Then we got a 'good boy', a kiss and sometimes a hug. 'You come, watch Daddy painting door white', not a hoax this time, just an excellent invitation to observe a genuine bit of DIY. And Daddy was very amused the day Tom learnt, 'perhaps'. At bedtime John said to him 'Goodnight, see you in the morning' and to his surprise back came the solemn, somewhat stylised sign 'Perhaps'! In October Tom told his first lie, convincing us he was going up to bed to sleep when, in fact, he crept up to Grannie's flat and begged another birthday chocolate!

Language was coming on really well. Questioned about a gorilla he proffered 'in my red book, upstairs on my bed'. And when he had to fetch Dan and a friend when it was time for the latter to leave he did so with a 'Hurry up, downstairs, bye-bye, Dan bed'. I doubt Daniel was very thrilled to be bossed around by his little brother in front of his schoolmate! And, no angel himself, when Tom suffered the indignity of falling off his cycle in full view of all his friends on the school bus, he vented his fury on the bike, the tree and me, and then lay on the kitchen floor for ten minutes, in tears of frustration and rage. But finally rallied and announced 'Crying finished!'

That autumn term was a time for rejoicing once we heard that the nursery at Darrick Wood had been reprieved and would remain open for hearing and deaf children. The good news, broken to me by a reporter, was not totally absorbed since it was clouded by the fact that two boys squabbling in the hall while I was on the phone had smashed a favourite jug of flowers, the water from which was slowly seeping through my shoes as I tried to frame a coherent quote for the paper! But it was my first taste of parent power . . .

Chapter 5
Good Times – Bad Times

When a child believes that he himself has something intensely loving to offer that will be accepted with love, and when at the meeting point of these two offerings a delight is formed, he comes naturally and healthily to communication, to stories, and, I believe, to writing and reading. (Leila Berg, 1977)

Just as abruptly as the peripatetic visits had ended, long before I felt ready, so did Tom's time in the nursery and it came as a shock when, rising five, he joined the reception class, where he was the second tallest pupil. How I longed, on his first day in the infants, to be taking him by the hand and depositing him at the school opposite our house, just like my local friends were doing with their offspring. To be unable to do so for a second time around sometimes seemed hard to bear. The deafness that denied me that pleasure also denied Daniel the privilege of playing the idolised 'big brother' in school and Tom the security of a reassuring sibling on hand. Meningitis has a lot to answer for in our family, as indeed in every family it touches, but at least Tom was not away at boarding school which I was all too aware is often a very real threat in areas where there is no suitable local provision for deaf children who need to sign.

Years later I was to count my blessings anew when I read artist Hamish Rosie's beautifully illustrated biography (*My Island – The True Story of a Silent Challenge*, 1999). Sent away from his island home to a school for the Deaf in Aberdeen at the unbelievably tender age of four years, Hamish's mother made a special plea for all his laundry to be returned to her each week. The familiar box containing it was to be *his* only tangible link with his parents during the long school term and *her* only chance to feel they were still a normal family as she watched his diminutive clothes dancing on the washing line. As I read that story my heart bled for that little boy and his sorrowful mother in the 1940s.

Although he was on familiar territory and with his friends from the old nursery class, it was a long day for Tom, with no midday nap as before, and he would often arrive home in fighting mood. A quick burst with his toy cars usually calmed him down. He would relax on the floor with his adored

Tom's serene smile said it all when he started at
the Primary HIU

'roadie' play mat and sometimes slink right underneath it, cleverly
allowing the contours of his body to make a landscape, then ease himself
out carefully, leaving the 'hills' to ensure maximum thrills and spills for his
toy cars.

Grannie, starting what was to become a four-year period of senile
dementia, was in hospital for Tom's fifth birthday but he visited her there
and was very fascinated by, and friendly towards, all the other patients in
the geriatric ward, even to the extent of ordering me to kiss the occupant of
the next bed! He enjoyed getting what we called Grannie's 'flattic' ready for
her return, spraying polish every time my back was turned, and was
delighted to find her safely ensconced upstairs on his return from school
two days later. The following interrogation took place when we were alone
that evening.

You and Grannie came walking home?
'No, Grannie came home in a little red car. Mummy waiting at home looking out of the window'.
T: (puzzled) Ambulance is white.
'This was a hospital lady's car' (not knowing the sign for occupational therapist).
T: (perking up, hopefully) Red car with flashing light on top?
'No, no light'.

Thomas then lost interest since it had become apparent to him that a dramatic drive was not unfolding. He contented himself by miming the doctor waving 'bye-bye' to Grannie and then returned, satisfied, to his colouring book.

With a hearing child I know this dialogue could hardly be counted worthy of note but deaf children are often known to be delayed in their questioning. Yet again it was signing, allied to his own lively curiosity, that was giving him the key to 'normal' conversation. It wasn't many months before he was continually querying 'What doing?', 'Where going?' or 'Who for?'

Rejoicing in him as we did, we discovered as a family that it was not Tom's *deafness* that made him different, it was his *food fads*. Despite a reputation as a fairly good cook whose offerings had always been appreciated by his brothers, my confidence in my culinary efforts was shaken when I found Tom was heavily into junk food! He did, however, enjoy helping in the kitchen and there were times when I was in a rush and dreaded him appearing just as I was about to make some hurried pastry, since I knew his insistence on helping would slow us down considerably. When we had some precious time to ourselves we were able to enjoy activities such as making meringues, marmalade, bread and Christmas puddings together and drew pictures, took photographs or cuttings from magazines to back up the experience and increase his vocabulary. Once, when his over-enthusiastic stirring of the dry pudding ingredients led to a proportion of them spilling on the floor, I indicated he should sweep them up. Turning back a few seconds later to see if he'd accomplished the task I was horrified to find him returning the contents of the dustpan carefully to the huge mixing bowl. With so many hours steaming ahead of it I was sure no ill effects would be incurred so I turned a blind eye – and lived to tell the tale! By the time he got to senior school this exposure to kitchen lore stood him in good stead in cookery lessons and he was able to get on with the tasks in hand without relying on support staff.

Reading Starts, Signing Changes

At last, to our delight, by May 1985 Thomas was starting to read in the unit and we were back on the 'Roger Red Hat, Billy Blue Hat' bandwagon for the third time around. It was noted that he 'takes great pride in his reading ability' and we could see that, when one was not available, he was making up his own signs. Confidence with words meant that he didn't take things at face value. For the first time he queried why I had said something, 'Why you say "hurry"?' He looked at the board at the swimming pool which had details of strokes/distances/medals and wanted to know what it said. Late for his lesson and not having time to explain in detail I took the easy way out and said I didn't know. He studied it long and hard and then came up with a neat answer. 'I think it says "Don't forget your pants"!'

By the end of term he seemed to have such an innate enjoyment of language he could devise his own game using his homework word cards from school. Spreading them out he instructed us to:

> Put the SAID under Dan's shoes, put the BED on the table, put the OUT under your bag, put the DARK in the cushion, put the OH under my little table, put the WITH by Dan's bottom (Dan sat *on* it and was promptly corrected), put the WHITE in my book, put the TWO by your skirt, put the WAS by the sofa, put the PULLED by my leg.

Family involvement with his learning let us all share in the fun, delighting us and best of all, I realise now, empowering him.

After two years of deliberation and discussion between professionals from several different disciplines, deaf adults and pupils' parents, Signed English was gradually being phased in to the unit and proved not nearly the ordeal I expected. Thanks to special training days on site, teachers and parents learnt it alongside each other and, like the children, seemed to take the switch-over from Paget Gorman in their stride and Tom soon learnt to use the possessive 's' in his writing. The grammatical markers showed these as well as past tenses and word endings such as 'ing' and 'ly'. He enjoyed the new signs for numbers and invented a game at home whereby he raffled all his toys and signed the winning numbers before handing them over!

In time the local Sensory Support Service and its units produced a series of Marathon sign dictionaries incorporating Signed English, British Sign Language and some local variations to which, as a consumer, I was proud to contribute variously as proof reader, researcher and sub-editor. With invaluable input from a deaf sign language tutor and her contacts in the Deaf community they became a wonderful resource and in due course smaller volumes with specialist senior unit signs for science and humanities were produced. At the present time, as part of a language project, professionally produced videos of the Signed English used at different stages in the primary unit are being used.

Using his ever increasing language skills to predict the future, at the end of the 1985 summer holidays Tom speculated on the forthcoming transport. 'I think same old bus again'! The beloved 'boo buth' of his early years seemed to have lost its appeal at last. One of the first things they worked on at school in year two was the verb 'to let'. 'Let me see your hand', he demanded, and 'Let me have your pillow'. He also enjoyed the power it gave him. 'I let you go now', he signed as the bedtime story came to an end. Although I didn't realise it at the time, in retrospect it seems to me that any control Tom could have via language was so valuable. The fact that he used it so graciously was an added and unexpected bonus.

With his brothers growing up and with his own penchant for small people, around this time Tom decided he needed a new playmate. Despite the fact that I had told him his main-school teacher was growing a baby in her tummy (which he flatly denied) he came to me bearing a piece of paper on which he had written 'I saw baby Lucy on "Blue Peter"', advising me '*You* go shopping for a new baby!' Alas, he didn't find one in his Christmas stocking but by January 1986 he could already project himself forward and ask how long before Christmas would come again, putting in an order for his presents in good time. 'Me 'ave a trumpet or a trombone'!

I taught Tom the expression 'oh dear' for reasons which now escape me but which must have seemed appropriate at the time. A few days later, in the car, I thought how sweet and clever of him to remember it when he tapped me on the shoulder, giggled and signed and said it. Ten minutes later, when we reached home, I realised why. He'd wet his dungarees! Despite being constantly told that deaf children had poor memory, Tom's often seemed excellent. After Christmas he stressed, when looking at a Nativity picture in a book 'Remember Mary was very, very tired on the donkey' and '2000 years ago a very real Jesus was borned'. He had comments for everything. A heavy headed, drooping hyacinth on the dining table was described as 'a soldier, bowing'. He picked up the word 'rhubarb' which was to become his best vocalisation, especially when combined with his favourite 'crumble' and I defied anyone to misunderstand his rendition!

New Language Strategies

Suzanne, his teacher in the unit. made the learning of prepositions fun by her class acting them out via the book *Bears in the Night* by Stan and Jan Berenstain (1972). Tom loved this activity and proved to me two months before his sixth birthday how much he had absorbed when I produced a pack of LDA (Learning Development Aids) preposition cards (photographs of models in everyday settings) which he'd never seen before. He immediately turned them into a brilliant game in which he himself was performing all the actions and, although I'd have preferred it in much shorter bursts, he insisted on going through all 54 over the space of two consecutive evenings, with signs / words as a commentary, which I wrote down verbatim. When I read them now I still find it hard to believe, but the home / school book doesn't lie as to the date.

My favourite was 'I think I stand and wait for man in the loo' and the longest one was 'I am pushing very, very hard to make a funny big umbrella on the table' (picture of a woman erecting a sunshade over a garden table). He also added other asides such as, 'Be careful! I am walking over the bridge' and 'I am picking the baby up because the baby is crying' (and this added explanation was volunteered and not in answer to a query from me). 'I am going up into the window – I naughty boy!' 'I go up and then I go in the church' followed by 'I say "bye-bye God" and then I walk down the steps'. 'The baby is laughing to mummy in the pram'. 'I am looking through the window' and 'I am mending the television because the television is broken'.

Quite simply he was just a delight to be around. He had such a genuine enjoyment of the things we did with language. If he'd seen it as a chore or a bore, or I'd seen it as an activity that alienated us I'd have never forgiven myself. Our relationship was far too precious to jeopardise. I couldn't subscribe to the views of the avowed oralist speech therapist who wrote that it was much better to have some 'unpleasantness and deprivation' at four, five, six or seven years than the 'bitter frustration of a lifelong handicap'. I could envisage a lifelong handicap of frustration and damaged relationships being far worse than an inability to articulate beautifully. But then the writer had already dismissed deaf children as frequently being 'wayward, demanding, restless and immature' although she did concede that they could overcome problems to eventually become 'almost as normal as other human beings'. It was obvious that we didn't speak the same language! (Mary Courtman-Davies, 1979).

Of course Tom didn't get everything right but somehow even his errors were endearing. On Mothering Sunday he bounced in to our bedroom, gave me a big hug, said 'Happy birthday' and presented me with an Easter egg! He had been meant to take part in a Mothering Sunday celebration at church but had been so wilful during the rehearsal I had withdrawn him and so, instead of feeling mellow and motherly during the service, I felt fed-up and furious, especially as the other children behaved like little angels.

As a sign of his advancing years Tom announced quite emphatically in the bath one night that he would no longer be deaf when he was seven or eight. Despite the sudden stab to my heart, fortunately I was prepared for this misconception since it is apparently a classic one and frequently born of the fact that the deaf youngster never sees deaf adults and therefore has no role models. Since, happily, this was not true for Tom I thought quickly and came up with the example of Lynda who was grown-up and still deaf but, on two positive notes which I knew would mean more to him than anything else at that moment, she is TALL and she DRIVES A CAR! He cheered up immediately and latched on to the idea of being a driver one day himself. For parents confronted by this evidence of questioning identity, the oralist therapist's advice, I discovered later, was to give a candid answer but point out that if the child works hard 'his speech will improve'. As if that were the only concern contained in a very complex situation!

The annual statement review at the age of six years and two months commented on Tom's grasp of English language as 'extremely good', the teachers noting that

> he uses language with meaning and purpose, often showing a delight-ful imagination and sense of humour. Most situations within school can be explained to him because he has a wide range of vocabulary and experience on which to draw.

To my delight I observed that he read better than a lot of top infants I'd heard at the local school where an identical reading scheme was used. Considering the circumstances I felt I could be forgiven a few smug feelings and a little parental pride in his prowess. We always tried to ensure he had as many new experiences as possible but some provoked an alarming reaction. The sport of fencing was one, when I took him to the mayor's fete at the local civic centre. He watched the display, entranced for a time, then became bored and signed 'Hurry up, kill!' at which point I realised, to my horror, that he was expecting the contestants to fight to the death, the bloodthirsty little wretch.

Other Senses Into Play

He may not have *heard* things as a point of reference but it seemed as if Tom stored up so many memories, even smells! Exactly one year after he had been to the zoo with his nursery class, we drove through some country lanes and encountered an overwhelming smell of farmyard manure. Before we could close the car windows Tom announced from the back seat 'I smell rhinoceros!'

The sense of sight was also important, of course, and he was very thoughtful in his observations. Watching a film on television about a 12-year-old undergoing an appendectomy, he explained to me that the curtains round the bed were because of 'nosey' people and was aware enough to spot that the youngster was speaking slowly because of her pain.

'Slow words' he said as he lip-read her. He insisted on watching the whole operation which made me wonder if it was a sadist or a wannabe surgeon we had in our midst.

Never one to use his deafness as an excuse, Tom was willing to be blind-folded at Junior Church one day when the term's collection was designated for the charity Guide Dogs for the Blind. Daniel was bursting with pride about his young brother when he got home, having overheard one of the group leaders say how brave Tom was to do it since it was so much harder for him than for the other children who could still rely on their hearing as they fumbled their way around the dauntingly large church hall.

He was very tactile, too. He helped himself to my bubble bath in heavy-handed fashion and ended up with a backside covered in white froth, resembling a ballet tutu. He saw the funny side and likened himself to a rabbit with a scut, or pom-pom tail as he called it! No wonder the unit said he was a pleasure to take out, interested in everything and soaking up information like a sponge.

On the rare occasions when I was able to be there, it lifted the heart to hear him in speech therapy although he said categorically, 'Me no like an oop and oof' which were the sounds he was currently working on. It must have been very difficult for him to understand the necessity for all the hard work that went into using a voice which he himself could not hear.

Although when he was a toddler I once awoke with such a sense of unbe-lievable joy from a dream in which he had been speaking clearly, I was in reality just happy that he used his voice without any prompting. Had he done so under duress it would have grieved me. I had already met some oral deaf adults who had been forced to speak as children and their voices all too often had a strangled sound I found painful to listen to. Not because of the *quality* but because of the strain it represented and their own acknowledged frustration that the joy of any early, easy communication via signs had been denied them.

The summer of 1986 heralded yet another carnival float for the local charity, Bromley Chain, and one for which we were awarded a coveted shield, with the children dressed as Buzzee Bees. I wrote to the local paper beforehand with a story about Tom's survival from meningitis six years previously and, since there was no opportunity for them to get their own photograph of him, I sent them one of the happiest I'd recently done of him taken, of all places, in the dentist's chair as part of my recording of regular events for the scrapbook! Walking home through Bromley after it had appeared on the front page I was stopped in my tracks by the billboard advertising the issue outside the paper's local office – 'Carnival joy for miracle boy' it read. It was with a very full heart and a huge sense of thanksgiving that I continued on our journey.

Back at school after the holidays he had a new teacher in the HIU for year three. Jacqui H found the way to his heart immediately. She let him sit beside her in her car in the school parking area and play with all the switches! Meanwhile, on the work front, with the change to Signed English I made him an a-b-c finger-spelling book with suitable magazine cuttings and also doctored his favourite Ladybird picture dictionary to include photocopies of the finger-spelling alphabet. (In an effort to improve deaf / hearing integration, the friend I was to make later in Sheffield produced and published one herself – *Learning Together ABC, A Finger-Spelling Alphabet with Signs for Deaf and Hearing Children* by Dorothy and Jacqui Dowling (1990) now about to be reprinted for the fourth time, followed by *Learning Together Finger-Spelling Cards* and two ABC charts.) Books still delighted Tom and brought out his own inventiveness. Encountering a cockatoo in a Topsy and Tim book he gave it his own unique description – 'a punk parrot' while a peacock displaying feathers became a 'fan bird'.

Integrated Experiences

It meant a lot to Tom to integrate with hearing youngsters, especially where sports or physical challenges were concerned. In his teens he was to tell a writer from the RNID *One in Seven* magazine that his best memories were the great times he'd had with hearing people doing judo, swimming, Scouts, youth club. His worst memory, it transpired, was 'Probably the day I started getting spots'. To me, his acne paled into insignificance compared with *my* worst memory of his young life but, thank God, that horror was something he could not recall.

At the age of seven years he was confident enough to take part for the first time in the Beckenham version of 'Super Stars' at the local sports centre where, after several days of events, including swimming, ball games and athletics, he was delighted to come third with the Bronze Award presented by the mayor. I had to go with him to sign at all the events, of course, and make sure he understood and followed instructions, and I often wondered if he would have done even better if he could have *heard* the spectators cheering the youngsters on. To compete in silence must be so strange it seems to me, as a hearing person, since crowd reaction is so encouraging. And, face down in the water or with his eyes fixed on the running track's finishing line, he couldn't see any wild gesticulations from me on the sidelines by way of encouragement.

Such was Tom's confidence and calm behaviour when occasion demanded, that he became a boat boy (bearing the incense in its little silver container) at St George's church, the first of our three boys to be asked to do so. Wearing a long white alb and rope belt he coped beautifully and

Tom proudly holding the silver 'boat' alongside
Katherine Conway, Joan and Steffen's daughter

proudly recorded the fact that he was now a 'boot (sic) boy' at church in his
news at school. No doubt the teachers thought that explained his
frequently black hands!

When he started judo he thoroughly enjoyed it although he appeared to
have not an ounce of aggression in him and seemed happy to lie back and
think of England! With so much confidence in coping among strangers,
even with the Japanese terms of judo, I was surprised and really saddened
when we were visiting our old friends in Petersfield and he wanted to play
with Sarah's collection of little erasers. I told him to go and ask her if he
might but he refused somewhat sadly with 'Sarah won't understand me'.
Even at seven his mature, realistic view of himself sometimes curtailed his
enthusiasm. The fact that it sapped his confidence was painful to me but I
respected his feelings and understood the reticence he showed in some
situations.

Fortunately his natural ebullience couldn't stay crushed for long. When

Signing '7' as Tom and John Hurd share a birthday

a new (hearing) pupil started in the juniors in September 1987 he was quite confident enough to write to him, no doubt enviously influenced by the fact that the parent drove a Rolls Royce. Tom's letter went 'Dear Boy, I will come to your birthday on . . . What your name? Love from Thomas'. It seemed as if Tom's confidence came via the written, rather than spoken word, and I fancy I know the source of that particular trait.

It was an exciting day for Tom when he and I went to nearby West Wickham hoping to see the Princess of Wales who was opening a Barnardo's Centre in what had been Matthew's old special school of St Nicholas. En route we bought a small Union Jack for Tom to hold and we stood and waited. The local paper's photographer snapped him waving his flag and he was quite the centre of attention, until two pretty little girls in velvet collared coats arrived whereupon his flag was 'borrowed' for them to use for a photocall. In the interests of equality his picture did appear as well! He was fascinated by the Princess and by the huge black limousine and especially the fact that she was seen to do something as ordinary as sneeze in it! I think the memory became quite poignant ten years later when she was to die in another black car as, after being in London for an FYD (Friends for Young Deaf People) meeting, he walked alone to see all the flowers at Buckingham Palace and came home very moved by the experience. Fearing the size of the anticipated crowds I didn't offer to accompany him to London on the funeral Saturday and we watched it instead on television. But afterwards I felt sad that I hadn't been brave enough to join the mourners as he himself regretted it and when I pointed out that, unlike me, he had at least seen some of the flowers and felt the atmosphere he replied sadly 'I know, but it wasn't enough'. I should have known better; first hand experiences were always the ones that held most meaning for him.

Coping with Change

Thomas had to adapt to many changes towards the end of 1987. My mother went into hospital again, hallucinating and sometimes becoming quite violent, making it impossible to leave her alone safely. Daniel G, the local deaf boy a little younger than Tom who, years later, was to be the 'inspiration' for Tom wanting a cochlear implant, moved to Sussex and I realised Tom didn't understand the implications and thought this was no different from a temporary, holiday home. We made up a scrapbook for him about moving house and all that it entailed, at which he became very envious and announced, 'I'm sorry. But, when I'm seventeen, I'm moving!' That didn't happen, I'm glad to say, and I don't know what it was in the intervening years that changed his mind, but at the time it was another instance when it was essential to act fast to make confusing events clear to a boy who had so much to learn and for whom everything had to be explained so graphically.

Lots more detailed explanations were soon required, since several other unsettling things were about to happen. Very early in 1988 his paternal grandmother died unexpectedly, in Hastings, while my own mother was still in Orpington Hospital. Brett, his close friend from the unit, left to go to board at a school for the deaf in Sussex, since his lovely young mother was terminally ill with cancer. Even Tom's godmother, Anne, moved away to Scotland with her family, which I duly signed for him. In total confusion he thought I meant she was moving to a chicken farm! (The sign for the former is based on the elbow action involved in playing bagpipes, not unlike our sign for chicken!) Teacher Jacqui H becoming engaged was a further cause for distress. Tom was heartbroken. 'I want to marry Miss H when I'm a man' he confessed. Luckily he promptly fell for someone at judo and was thereafter quite happy to lie on the floor in a hold, with a blissful smile, making no attempt to throw her off!

Since it was obvious that Thomas was getting nothing from his hearing aids, he tried something new – a vibro-tactile aid – on his wrist. At first it was declared 'magic' but his initial enthusiasm for it was very short-lived. But something he started on his eighth birthday *was* to continue for several

Sense of fun to the fore as 'waiter' Tom proffers
the gingerbread men he'd made

years – the Deaf Drama Club with Sarah Scott, the late comedian Terry
Scott's talented daughter. Tom took his deaf friends there for his birthday
treat and they had a great time at the Unicorn (Arts) Theatre off Leicester
Square in central London. To my surprise, there were only a couple of other
deaf children there which seemed a shame as hearing-impaired Sarah was
a brilliant teacher, with lyrical signing skills, and the subsidised Saturday
sessions such a fantastic opportunity to enrich their experience. Sometimes
parental apathy really bugged me.

Acceptance in deaf circles was important but, much as I wanted to, I
couldn't always help Tom over the inevitable heartaches that occurred
outside them. 'I saw lots of children go to Robert's party today. I think
Robert don't want me. I'm very sad' he said. For such a gregarious lad
being left out of a neighbouring boy's birthday celebrations really hurt but
luckily help was at hand in the shape of Caroline, eighteen months older
than him, who lived opposite and took him under her wing, communicating with written messages until such time as she, bless her, had picked
up his signs naturally. She introduced him to her friends around the area
and when mums and youngsters unknown to me greeted him when we
were out together it really warmed my heart. As he grew up it was
important to me that he had his own circle of friends and that I wasn't
always the one in control of his social scene.

At school Tom was reported as being

> a leader within the unit group and much respected by the other deaf children. He has a good sense of fun and can be involved in delightful imaginative play with them. He has made friends with hearing children.

Being in school so far from home and having no transport myself it was not easy for him to build on these latter friendships and socialise with classmates in the normal way, after lessons finished, and that was something else which worried and saddened me.

As soon as he was eight years old he started at Cubs, having longed for years to follow in his brothers' footsteps. Having them as role models must have helped him so much and it was a very starry-eyed boy who stood in front of Akela when he was ready to be invested. He threw himself heart and soul into all the activities, enjoying the badge work, the camps, the competitions, the camaraderie.

Quite rightly, Akela thought it would be a good idea for the Cubs to learn some signs for Tom's benefit so I was invited along to give them a demonstration. On our return home Tom told me 'I love you at Cubs; you look lovely. You beautiful signing'. With a lump in my throat I told him 'That's because I love you, Tom'. He pondered for a moment then 'Did you want me to be deaf?' he asked. I explained about praying to God to make him better and to get strong when he was so very ill as a baby, and that He had done just that. An evasive explanation, maybe, but it was about all I could manage at that moment. And if I were to search my heart now I wonder exactly what I would say. Did I want him to be deaf? No I didn't – but then even less did I want him to be *dead*. Deafness was the price *he* paid for survival but if it has contributed to the lovely person he is then I can only accept and embrace it. And what it brought in its wake – the people, the support, the insights into other lifestyles, the involvement, the experiences, have enriched my own life and given it a new direction and dimension.

It was good to see the way Tom coped with lessons at the local indoor pool. At times he seemed fearless, diving to the bottom to pick up not one but two bricks simultaneously, much to the concern of the mother beside me. In view of later developments I might not, myself, have been quite so relaxed about his long resurfacing time, had I known what was to overtake him before the year was out. In the holidays he obtained his Silver Challenge Award for swimming and, shortly afterwards, the 1500 metre badge. Although they were done locally these achievements were also celebrated in school, when awards such as these were shown and acknowledged in assembly. This served to raise the profile of the deaf pupils and to make it clear to the rest of the school that they could have the same skills as their peers. Lack of hearing did not need to be a stumbling block.

It had always seemed something of a duty and a joy to me to be alert to Tom's thoughts and try and anticipate his reactions. On Palm Sunday 1989 he was serving in church and, as boat boy, would be leading the procession alongside the senior server swinging the thurible with its incense. Traditionally on this one Sunday the long procession, complete with clergy and choir, would lead the congregation right round the outside of the big building, along the road and through the churchyard. Since we had arrived it had started to rain and I realised the outside walk would be abandoned. As they came down from the chancel steps I was signing frantically to Tom so that he would realise the change of plan which he wouldn't, of course, have overheard in the vestry line-up. I had a vision of him heading off in the wrong direction or having an altercation with his partner about the correct route! True to form he got the message on that occasion and it was not long before he was ready to be promoted to a 'torch' (carrying a candle) in which role he stayed further back in any procession, until such time as he graduated over the years through acolyte to crucifer with the big cross, and finally to thurifer himself, in charge of a small boat boy/girl.

Despite his own apparent fitness Tom was always concerned for others less fortunate. He was intrigued by a small girl in hospital on the television news. I explained that she had leukaemia and needed a bone marrow transplant to make her better. From his incredulous expression I knew he'd not understood. 'A bow and arrow to make her better?' he queried, miming a graphic description of a doctor in the guise of Robin Hood! Lip-reading is not infallible and there are some words for which there are either no known signs or they are not yet in *our* repertoire.

Areas of Concern

Always acutely aware of the world around him, at a time when environmental issues were much to the fore, Tom thoughtfully studied the sparks from a train at the points and asked, 'Do trains hurt the world?' And, instead of complaining about the bad insect bites he'd acquired in the garden he simply said 'I feel sad with myself'.

Tom was soon to have something which made us *all* sad, when a late legacy of the meningitis manifested itself. At the end of April 1989 the unit reported that he had complained of a poor head, gone very white and described it as a 'bad dream' when doing his spellings. As I read the words in the home/school book I felt uneasy but, never one to over-react, I told myself it couldn't possibly be what had flashed through my mind. Surely not *epilepsy?* I even joked about it, teasing him that some people will do anything to get out of a spelling test! But the episode was reported when he had his school medical the following day and the doctor said that she didn't like the sound of it. We ourselves thought no more of it.

During the summer holidays we were swimming as a family at West Wickham pools when he came up to me and asked me if he had gone white. Because, he explained, he had been looking at a man with a boy sitting on the side and felt he had seen it all happen before. Without *his* level of language and *my* understanding how would he have been able to explain this sense of *déjà vu* and how would we have known what was happening to concern him? We took him to our GP who checked him over thoroughly and felt there was no cause for alarm – 'One swallow doesn't make a summer' – but said he would refer him, in view of his medical history, to a neurologist at Guy's Hospital in London.

In the meantime the holidays progressed without further incident. Tom went to a YMCA day camp in the countryside at Westerham, about eight miles away, and had a wonderful week, despite being the only deaf youngster there and knowing only a few other participants. In activities such as this his confidence was amazing and much appreciated and applauded by the volunteers who were not used to deaf youngsters. He also enjoyed some adventure days away with the Cubs. All in all it was an action-packed summer before a sad autumn arrived.

Tom's appointment at Guy's with a neurologist was scheduled for September. Like our GP he didn't suspect anything wrong but said he would arrange for a 'non-urgent' brain scan to be done. I took that to mean we would have some months to wait and wasn't unduly concerned. Ostriches have nothing on me!

My Mother died on 17 October 1989, the evening before my fiftieth birthday. Although it was a merciful release it was a very stressful time, following a protracted period of visiting her in the nursing home nearly every day. The week of her cremation was half term and started with the Cub Cyclo Cross in which Tom was desperate to take part. In the previous ten days he had been awarded his Gold Challenge swimming badge, done 26 lengths in a sponsored swim for the Church Urban Fund, acted the part of a punk rocker in psychedelic wig for the school assembly, attended Cubs, Adventurers (the church youth group) and a party. Our energy levels were at a very low ebb.

Before we went to the crematorium on a beautiful autumn day Tom drew me a lovely picture of a hearse (bearing an uncanny resemblance to a stretch limo!) and coffin, flowers, undertaker, church with bell, cross and stained glass windows, gravestones, huge crucifix and a waiting priest. It bore the words 'This is to help stop you crying at church'. Unexpectedly,

Pachelbel's 'Canon', always so very meaningful to me, was being played as we arrived at the little chapel and I knew everything would be alright. I signed the service for Tom; I think it helped me and Father William, the assistant curate covering an interregnum at St George's, treated us very sensitively. My mother was a loner and although Tom queried, 'Lots of people coming? Did Grannie have any friends when she was a girl?' there were only the five of us there.

Afterwards we spent a reflective time looking at all the other flowers outside and Tom was intrigued by a small blue wreath which I explained was for a baby. Later that evening as we were finishing supper he turned to me and asked, oh so gently, 'Please don't cry about my question. But why did the *baby* die'? He could accept that frail Grannie's days were over at nearly 94 but couldn't understand a baby's demise. The sensitive way he phrased and prefaced his question made tears inevitable, but they were mostly ones of joy . . .

The remainder of half term passed in a daze, with a visit to our first subtitled film 'Johnno' at the National Film Theatre, after which Tom took to the stage with Mary Guest of the charity Sense, and was interviewed, signing and finger-spelling his school, name, and so on. There was also Deaf Drama Club at the weekend and I was on duty that Sunday in Junior Church. I was offered the chance to swap but felt I should do it and 'offer it up' for my mother since it would have been her birthday. Emotionally drained and physically exhausted I planned to do absolutely nothing for the rest of the day. Little did I know . . .

We were planning to make a wormery to give a new slant to the story of creation and lifecycles. Armed with buckets of soil and countless other essentials Tom and I arrived at the church hall early in the morning and I photographed the children as they helped make the wormery. Tom was very pensive but I thought either he was just feeling jealous that he wasn't receiving my full attention or he was still feeling sad about grannie. Another leader had taken along a beautiful book, *Beginnings and Endings with LIFETIMES in Between* by Bryan Mellonie and Robert Ingpen (1983) but I was unable to read it out loud to the children, as planned; my feelings were simply too raw at that time.

As we cleared up at the end of the long session I was aware that Tom wasn't looking too well but just at that moment I became embroiled in a discussion with a barrister friend questioning me about cued speech (an aid to vocalisation which is used with some deaf children) and by the time I extricated myself Tom was looking distinctly strange. His eyes were fixed at a point above my head and he was completely unresponsive. Luckily John was outside with the car and we bundled Tom in and drove home fast.

Once there he remained in the same state so we phoned for a doctor and were told to take him to Sydenham Children's Hospital.

Thomas, it seemed, had pre-empted the 'non urgent brain scan' and had a fully-fledged seizure. I couldn't believe it. Naïvely I had imagined that, having survived meningitis, he would somehow lead a charmed life and nothing else bad could befall him. Also, some time before she became so disorientated my mother had fallen asleep one afternoon and when I gently woke her had been quite strange, saying she had felt she'd died but had said to herself 'Oh good, Tom will be all right now'. I presume she thought she would somehow intercede for him, I don't know. It was a fairly spine-chilling moment at the time and must have stayed at the back of my mind, since I recalled it when she died. I didn't, of course, expect to see any change in Tom, but neither did I expect to see a deterioration like this, which so reminded me of the time we spent in hospital during the meningitis. From Daniel's stricken expression as he watched over his brother I knew he, too, was feeling very shaken.

We spent a miserable and worrying two days on a busy ward where parental friction among other families seemed ever ready to flare up, so different from our time alone in Farnborough Hospital. We were sent from Sydenham to Guy's Hospital early on the following Tuesday, driving through the worst of the rush-hour traffic for what we were told would be a brain scan. On arrival it transpired no such test was booked and nothing could be done that day. Tom was prescribed Tegretol (carbamazapine) tablets and we were sent on our way. The uncertainty of the exact problem and the fear of something more sinister than epilepsy was always at the back of my mind. The delays we were expected to face, both in the testing and in being told the results, would have been intolerable had John and I been born worriers.

Tom returned to school and all our friends were devastated at this latest turn of events. John Hurd wrote 'it's not fair!' But commented, 'Tom is quite impressive – considering his recent history. I was surprised to see him back at school, looking very poised and with-it'. It was only a matter of days before Tom was keen to be back as a torch on the servers' rota at church and nine days later returned to Guy's Hospital for an EEG (electro encephalo-gram) with which he coped admirably, pretending he was having a 'perm', smiling calmly all the way through and so relaxed he fell asleep. Thanks to Matthew having the same test at a young age, after a febrile convulsion, I had been able to prepare Tom for the procedure beforehand. (Over the years we had quietly worked our way through nearly all the excellent Althea picture books (Dinosaur Publications) – *Having an Eye Test, Having a Hearing Test, Going into Hospital, I Can't Talk Like You, I Have Epilepsy* although, to Matthew's chagrin, none of the three boys ever had the chance

Taking it in his stride – Tom stays unfazed by his
first EEG

to emulate the little chap on crutches with a plastered leg shown on one
page. I think he felt positively cheated but, since we'd encountered more
than our fair share of the other problems illustrated in the books, I was only
too happy to give this particular calamity a miss!)

Although the brain scan which followed was normal, thank God, the
EEG proved to be very abnormal, with a lot of activity, particularly when
asleep. The diagnosis of epilepsy was confirmed. Obviously it was an overwhelming relief that it wasn't a brain tumour but even so it felt to me that
yet another label had been slapped on to Tom, something he really didn't
deserve and could well have done without.

The neurologist we saw on our next visit to Guy's appeared unable to
appreciate just how sensible he was being about the condition. His
deafness seemed to faze her. She dismissed his 'funny dream' when he had
awoken pale, nauseous and headachy, as something we all have, irrespec-
tive of the fact that that was the way he used his limited language to
describe the attacks. Occasionally I had to remind him to take his pills but
he observed sadly, 'These are not making my brain better. I wonder why?'

Tom may have been on strong medication, may have been having bad
turns, but they didn't extinguish his lovely personality. Still true to his

fairly faddy eating habits, he eyed with great suspicion the blackcurrant pie I'd made one day and indicated that he didn't want any. I said I thought he should at least try a little before deciding he didn't like it. Reluctantly he accepted a small portion and, before tasting it, signed himself with the sign of the Cross. It is something I've seen other deaf people do, especially when about to do something they consider risky, so I was rather annoyed. When he demolished the lot and promptly passed his plate for a second helping I put it to him that maybe he should say sorry to me, for hurting my feelings at first. He duly apologised then thought for a long moment before solemnly announcing, 'I think *you* hurt the priest's feelings when you go to Communion', indicating me making the sign of the Cross before receiving the Bread and Wine. I was at first speechless, then helpless with laughter. It was a delight to discover that our deaf son could have the last word – and with such style.

Still pale and dark eyed at the packed Christmas Candlelit Carol Service, Tom was promoted from being an exuberant little shepherd of previous years to a proud young pageboy bearing the 'frankincense'. His king just happened to be a high profile city financier, behind whom Tom dutifully plodded as he every now and again stopped to point majestically to the imaginary star above the tableau representing Mary, Joseph and the Baby. Tom followed confidently before suddenly tapping his king smartly between his gold encrusted shoulders and pointing to another imaginary star in quite the opposite direction, determined it seemed to add his own interpretation to the biblical events!

Despite all he had been through it was wonderful to see he was still his own person and, as ever, able to make us smile!

Chapter 6

Coping and Caring

God understands every human language. Remaining close to him in silence is already prayer: your lips remain closed but your heart is speaking to him. And, by the Holy Spirit, Christ prays in you more than you can imagine. (Brother Roger of Taizé, 1991).

Following the EEG and brain scan, blood and eye tests at Guy's Hospital towards the end of 1989 Tom's dosage of carbamazapine was increased and had the effect of slowing him down, especially where maths were concerned. He still complained of headaches, nausea and the occasional 'funny dream' but was exasperated about the restrictions put on some of his activities. When told he must be supervised by me at Cub swimming sessions he was highly indignant and tried to strike a deal, 'If I have my epilepsy I'll get out of the water and if I die the man will telephone you.' There was really no answer to such reasoning but, of course, I went anyway! In his own inimitable style he finally accepted the limitations his condition imposed on him and even had the grace to say 'Thank you for coming to look after me'. He was also forbidden to cycle on the road but, because of the deafness, this was already out of the question as far as we were concerned.

Some nursing staff at Farnborough Hospital still remembered Tom from the 1980 episode and on his annual check-up with the consultant paediatrician were impressed at his progress but, like us, saddened by the latest setback he'd suffered.

Despite yet another mix-up with the long awaited appointment at the Phoenix Centre at Farnborough, eventually Tom was seen there by the doctor from Guy's Hospital. She was pleased that the relatively low dose of carbamazepine was keeping him free of fits which led her to think that he had a mild form of epilepsy and may well be able to come off medication in two years' time if no more seizures occurred. She explained that doctors tend to look at the child rather than at the EEG results (to me this sounded just like the experts looking at the *child* rather than the audiogram in deafness). So much advice in books on epilepsy seemed to mirror that in books on childhood deafness, so when reading them I felt we were travelling down a familiar road, albeit one I hadn't chosen to tread again. The only really painful thing for me to read was the advice to 'carry on talking' because the sufferer can still hear during a seizure and the sound of a voice can be reassuring. When Tom was fitting, with his eyes fixed, he couldn't focus on us to even benefit from our signs and that made me feel doubly sad. In time the headaches and pallor which continued to assail him every now and again were frequently found to be episodes of migraine which were rather clouding the issue when we were all understandably on tenterhooks about epileptic seizures.

At school, a major part of the term's topic in January 1990 was focused on whales and Inuit, with which Tom became really fascinated. He asked me one day if I knew where Inuit babies went and was starry-eyed when I confessed my ignorance and he had to enlighten me. 'In the boot! Yes, it's true!', and drew me an enchanting little sketch of the footwear to prove it. He made up his own sign for harpoon based not on what it did but on how it *sounded*. He could get his tongue round the word 'blubber' just beautifully and when the time came for his birthday, after he and his peers had been with the school to the Museum of Mankind and also seen a play about whales at the National Theatre, it was a simple matter to make an igloo birthday cake to continue the theme.

Despite the new health concerns Tom continued to take a keen interest in all his outside activities like Cubs, the newly joined karate and Adventurers, whilst still being very observant about what went on around him. Watching me make chicken stock one evening he commented 'Funny thing to make soup with – bones! Do they melt?' And in the middle of a crowded pathology lab waiting room, much to the fascination and amusement of the other patients, I had to explain to him the difference between 'face' and 'faeces', which he'd seen printed on a form he had to hand in! Such are the joys of a visual sign language, all in the cause of communication! To discover in the year 2001 that, according to the National Deaf Children's Society, 80% of parents never learn how to communicate effectively with their deaf child is something that desperately saddens me.

Transport Issues

Thinking ahead to Tom's future schooling, it had occurred to me that there was no evidence of transport being provided for the senior deaf pupils. That surprised me greatly, given that, at that time, those bright pupils awarded highly coveted places at Bromley's two super-selective schools, also in Orpington, were automatically bussed in, since many of them lived across the borough and well outside the catchment areas. Being profoundly deaf, of course, and having no option but to attend Darrick Wood school with its HIU, our child would have no choice but to make the journey alone, since his deaf peers lived on different routes.

Because the policy for the seniors was to insist that their deaf pupils travelled in under their own steam solely, it seemed, in the interests of increasing independence and not as any cost-cutting exercise, I took issue with it. It was painful to have to do so, especially as its instigator appeared to be John Hurd, supporting the wishes of the unit teaching staff. What seemed ludicrous to me was the fact that my near neighbour's bright young daughter should have almost door-to-door transport provided free while Tom, when the time came, was to be given a travel allowance and expected to catch four buses a day for the privilege of attending school. I had no wish to see school transport provided *ad infinitum* but I did feel that there would be enough to cope with at the start of senior school without the added stress of long, lonely bus journeys across the borough twice a day.

Parents of less deaf youngsters due to move up before Tom were also concerned and before long another campaign was under way. I hated having to disagree with people like John and upset the professional/ personal relationship we had established over those very precious early years, but I felt strongly about the safety and wellbeing of the Year 7s and 8s. And I know he felt equally strongly and had what he saw as very valid reasons for them relinquishing the transport. I like to think our respect for each other remained, despite the differences in opinion, and we could even joke about it when I suggested John thought maybe I'd given Tom lessons in epilepsy in order to make a stronger case for the retention of his transport! (Years later, when Tom took off to Borneo to cycle for charity I felt he had proved that the fact he was bussed to school at a critical time had not led to him becoming a perpetual wimp, devoid of any independence, as we'd been led to believe.)

Leaving aside the trauma of the epilepsy, we felt as parents that the fact that our children could not hear (e.g. questions, instructions, advice from bus drivers, passengers, pedestrians, and so on) could be a problem, especially if they failed to respond to a warning, change of route, lightning bus strike. In a crisis they would be unable to make telephone calls (this was in the days before nearly every schoolchild carried a mobile and sent text messages *ad nauseam!*) and could not hear traffic noises, not even those caused by emergency services' vehicles. The National Deaf Children's Society had already stated that a deaf child was three times as likely to be involved in a road traffic accident. A lack of clear speech might mean they could not be understood asking for advice, directions or help. Despite the borough's buzz-word being 'independence' I felt, as a parent, that the word 'discrimination' came more readily to mind. We felt there would be little to

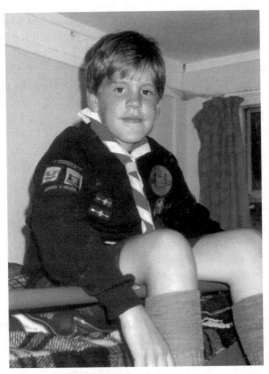

Outside activities meant a lot to Tom. Here he's
preparing to enjoy his first Cub camp

be gained by solitary, exhausting and unnecessary journeys across the
borough on public transport, but a lot to be lost.

As parents we all strove to make our children independent in our own
way. Ours was by integrating Tom in many outside activities. Were he to be
spending even more hours travelling each day these would have to be
curtailed or cancelled, since he would have little time or energy to partake
in these extra activities after school and would be likely, we felt, to become
more isolated rather than more independent.

Eventually the Education Committee accepted recommendations from
an Assistant Educational Director and there was a change in policy by 1990.
In future it was agreed that the subject should be raised at each pupil's
annual review when factors such as the complexity of the journey, medical
and compassionate grounds should be taken into account. Even so, at the
time of Tom's final statement review in the junior school there was still a
suggestion that he should be using public transport at some point during
his first year at secondary stage. With the profound hearing loss and its

Proud of his Gold Arrow certificate in Cubs

attendant communication difficulties, epilepsy, and migraine, we felt this was still unacceptable, a viewpoint endorsed by his consultant and our GP. Tom eventually travelled independently in Year 9 once the treatment for epilepsy was withdrawn and during that time it was interesting to me to note that parents who had not supported the campaign were the very ones who were protectively driving their offspring to senior school every day themselves!

In November 1990 Tom was awarded the Gold Arrow at Cubs, a very proud moment for him in the Church Hall. At that time I was running the Toddler Group in the same hall and later that month one of its very small members, an only child of friends from St George's, was knocked down by a car outside his home and died later in the Maudsley Hospital. We were all devastated and Tom knew something was wrong as soon as he got in from school. I explained the sequence of events to him and he obviously thought long and hard about them. He was unable to go to bed until he had found a photograph of himself with the little chap, taken at Junior Church in the hall only a few weeks beforehand. He mounted it on a piece of paper and then wrote down as much as he could remember of what I had told him, not 100% accurately, and added his own sad feelings. Just as this book has been for me, I suspect it was very therapeutic for him to get his thoughts on paper immediately so that he could remember little Matthew. I told him that I thought all the happy feelings would have gone for his parents and he sadly agreed, saying/signing thoughtfully 'Now they have empty life'. His sensitivity and compassion seemed quite exceptional for one so young.

So Much For Subtitles

In the run up to Christmas Tom seemed surprised to see me engrossed in a Delia Smith programme on television. 'Are you interested to watch TV about how to cook food?' he queried. He was intrigued by the word 'bangers' for sausages and wondered if it came from a 'different country?' Subtitled television programmes like this led to so much language acquisition although occasionally the scrambled captions made little sense.

On one occasion we were watching a programme together about the RAF pilots lost for many days in the Borneo jungle. A mention was made of cannibalism and I suspected Tom would need this word explained to him. Watching out for it in the fractionally delayed subtitles, so that I could draw his attention to it, I was distinctly amused to see it appear as 'inter-ballistic missile' rather than 'cannibalistic'! Tom summed up some of the oddities which slip through in subtitling and frequently exasperate me, 'Yeah, sloppy talking, like sloppy signs, I say'. I do appreciate that subtitling is not an exact science and that it is not the same as normal typing but there's no real independence for a deaf viewer if someone has to be on hand to interpret the erroneous subtitles too often!

Shortly before Christmas, antihistamines were prescribed for Tom's migraines which made him even more drowsy over the holiday, and in the New Year he started an elimination diet from the hospital to see if there were any specific triggers. He took this very seriously and was conscientious about sticking to it, regardless of all the post-Christmas parties, and scrutinising labels carefully in the supermarket. True to form he chose to put back fried foods into his diet at the earliest opportunity, simply so he could partake of crisps and fish and chips! Cheese came next which meant he could reintroduce chocolate just in time for Easter. No definite cause was ever identified and, happily, in time the migraines, which were preceded by a red aura, disappeared. Like the epilepsy they seemed to coincide with a sudden growth spurt at puberty when for the first time he could no longer wear his brothers' hand-me-downs since the waists would go nowhere near him.

Some New Experiences

In the Easter holidays 11-year-old Tom spent five consecutive days at the Unicorn Theatre, in a dream-maker play, written by a nine-year-old from Dulwich, South London. Sarah Scott had arranged for Tom and another deaf boy from her drama group to join the hearing youngsters but, due to unforeseen circumstances, she was away herself and I had to stay to sign the story and stage directions for Tom. I enjoyed feeling so involved with the development of the play and so fascinated by watching the 30 young thespians that I couldn't tear myself away when Sarah eventually returned.

The play's dream-maker had raging toothache and sent to earth for the Famous Five to cure his pain. Tom was in a 'Toothache Rap', sporting long, green 'germ' fingers as he attacked the molars and giant toothbrush with a suitable grimace! In the dream sequence he was a footballer in a playground scene and a clown in the circus. When the dream-maker stirred all sorts of unmentionables into a magic potion Tom and all the cast *signed* the key words to the song – his contribution being a suitable mime/sign/gesture for 'squashy eyeball' (best not to go into details!) My favourite part was when he played a kangaroo with bouncy hops to Benjamin Britten's 'Simple Symphony'. Tom's 'West End debut' in the Unicorn's gala day, in the presence of Angharad Rees and other celebrities, was a fun new experience and one which, after he got over his initial surprise and irritation that once is not enough and scenes have to be practised again and again, he really enjoyed.

The junior school's traditional trip to the Isle of Wight during the pupils' last term was a learning curve which Tom took in his stride and, despite wretched weather, he enjoyed the experience of being away. He was fascinated by Osborne House and, as part of that project, was required to write a letter from Queen Victoria to her daughter. For once his usual sensitivity deserted him. He wrote:

Dear Vicky,
I am your mother, Queen Victoria. I have got a bad news for you. Your father died.

Final Report

The end-of-term report spoke of Thomas's continuing good progress with language acquisition. It was noted that he used complex sentences with confidence, absorbed and used new vocabulary and idiomatic phrases in all situations and his question forms and more complex grammatical structures were reflected in his written work. The medication for migraine had upset his concentration and speed in maths but he was regaining some confidence. Despite his recent difficulties he had continued to 'relate to the other children with patience, kindness and general thought-fulness.'

In the main school his drama was summed up in a comment about his 'very good mime skills, drawing on own extensive experience to develop some excellent work'. I thought back to John Hurd's comment about this very subject, in his pre-nursery letter, some eight years beforehand. The Senior Educational Psychologist added her comments

> Thomas is a boy who has a relaxed and pleasant manner. He is a socia-ble, stable child who relates well to his peer group and the adults around him. He is able to take part in drama in a London setting and to join in all the Church activities within his own community.

With his good average intellectual ability on the practical tests of intelli-gence she felt that socially, emotionally and academically he would be well placed in the Senior Hearing Impairment Unit at Darrick Wood.

Since, according to the NDCS, 40–50% of deaf children have emotional, behavioural and adjustment disorders (compared to 25% of children in the general population) in retrospect, this professional observation is very encouraging and proof to me, yet again, that good communication is a key to normal development.

Thomas and his other deaf peers visited the senior school, some few hundred yards up the road from the primary one, and Jackie Parsons, head of the HIU there, with typical foresight, made a video of them discussing their future expectations and ambitions. Andrew, Tom's Greek Cypriot friend, was seen earnestly explaining that he was going to work very, very hard and do his homework. Whereas Tom, nonchalantly leaning back in his chair, appeared to be planning to do nothing more than aspire to a Porsche and a Ferrari one day!

I knew Tom would miss the old unit very much, especially as he had, somewhat inadvisedly I felt, in view of the fact that he would soon have to experience many different subject teachers, had the same teacher of the deaf for three consecutive years. With fewer children in the new unit he realised it was much smaller. He told me about a boy who was joining them there from a different junior school. His parents were deaf and when I imparted this information to Tom he asked how I knew. 'Because Mrs Parsons signed for them at the meeting', I explained. He digested this news then declared 'I am lucky.' 'Why?' I queried. 'Because my parents are not deaf'. I felt very moved by that since it spoke volumes about our life. It could have been so easy for Tom to long to be part of a completely deaf family if we had been unable to communicate with him.

By the end of that final term we had amassed no fewer than 33 home/school exercise books, which have since become a joy to read, serving to remind me of incidents and, sometimes, people long forgotten. They also bring home to me the fact that Tom's brothers figured in the equation just as much as he did. At times it seemed I was having to be in three places at once, juggling school and hospital appointments, reviews, medicals, signing classes, sports days at opposing ends of the borough, by day, swimming lessons, Judo classes, committee meetings and the like by night, and trying to keep the whole family fed and happy in the process. I know I was lucky to be able to be a 'full time' mum but I did note ruefully in one entry that Tom was entranced by playing a challenging 'Game of Life' board game we'd been given. 'With one like ours,' I scribbled, 'who needs a *game?*'

I found it sad to be reliably informed recently that it is unlikely any family today would be allowed to retain such memorabilia. And the reason? Because a stray remark about a pupil's prowess in primary school could become cause for litigation at secondary stage if a parent feels a promised potential has not been fully realised. Be that as it may, the two-way contact spanning 25 school terms was so vital to Tom's well-being and to my sanity. Re-reading them now brings home to me that, in a way, every passing phase of childhood is like a little bereavement. Where is he now, that endearing little chap who made us laugh – and cry with joy – and count our blessings?

My last ever entry in the home/school book was dated 24 July 1991 and focused, not for the first time, on food! The previous Sunday, after a big lunch, Tom had asked what was planned for supper. When he was told it would be only an apple and some cheese he gave an old-fashioned look and commented sourly, 'I think we're living in Victorian times. Only a little food and drink!' A final entry about an obviously deprived child of the eighties.

Chapter 7

Growing Up

It is a pleasure to have Thomas in the school and a privilege to teach him. (*Jackie Parsons, Head of Senior Hearing Impairment Unit, October 1991*)

On 3 September Tom started at Darrick Wood Senior School, looking very grown up in his brown jacket and trousers and yellow shirt. Home/ school exercise books were now a thing of the past and his pride in his new, pocket-sized contact book is evident in the lovely snapshot we have of him proudly showing it to his tall brother, who was himself just entering the sixth form of the local Langley Park Boys' School. Yet again I couldn't help reflecting what a joy it would be for both boys to be at the same school, setting off together, sharing the 20-minute walk and some of the same experiences.

But Tom was destined to cope alone. And cope he did. By half term he had the kudos of that contact book containing effort grades 1 for nine subjects, and effort grades 2 for three subjects, one of those being music. He had, it seemed, made a good start in his new school and settled well into the routine. Fortunately, Susie, his form tutor in the main school, was herself a qualified teacher of the deaf and we were very blessed that Jackie, the Head of Unit, had already become a friend since we had met at the primary unit signing classes and then collaborated on the sign dictionaries which the Sensory Support Service was producing.

Jackie herself has a deaf daughter and I think listening to the talk I had written and taped about bringing up a deaf child really struck a chord with her. It was, she told me, the first time she had heard anyone give voice to the sort of feelings and experiences with which she, too, could identify so closely. With so many shared experiences there can't help but be a unique bond of understanding between some parents and strong friendships serve as a source of support as well as, frequently, a genuine delight.

The talk had been written, several years earlier, at the request of the primary unit, to be given to a Methodist women's group considering making a donation towards books for the deaf pupils. I started off with a 'yellow is a lovely word to see' piece (see Appendix 1) which had been written when Tom was just one year old, at a time when I felt not only over-whelmed by what lay ahead of us but also very positive about it, too. In many ways it had been very therapeutic for me to *write* down and sort out my thoughts but, bringing it out for public consumption seven years later, I had to practise *reading* some parts aloud many times before I could do so without an uncontrollable wobble in my voice and tears in my eyes. The remainder of the talk covered areas which I hoped might make anyone unfamiliar with childhood deafness stop and think of some of its surprising implications for day-to-day living. But, because of my good fortune and delight in Tom, it was all in such a very upbeat mode that I felt I had better recap towards the end with some of the undoubted downsides, in order to elicit and warrant the desired donation! Since that time I've repeated it, suitably updated, to many different groups, in many different venues. It still never ceases to amaze me that I have the courage to stand up and talk about things so personally meaningful, since in the 1970s as a Fashion Editor I had stubbornly maintained that even doing a commentary for a clothes show would be totally beyond my capabilities! So strange to find that the life of a small, dear son had brought out a new and unknown confi-dence in me.

And in the same way having him had brought home to me that the need for *communication* should overcome any qualms or inhibitions. I discovered this when we were able to find respite care for my mother and at last take Tom, aged six years, on his first ever family holiday away from home. Our rented *gite* in Normandy was in a country hamlet where little English was spoken. Instead of my normal reticence to dredge up my fairly pathetic schoolgirl French I found myself chatting away, probably with a million mistakes a minute, because I cared more about *contact* than about being word perfect. At least I got '*Il est sourd*' right when small blond Tom caught the eye of a local veteran who invited us to his home, presented him with a precious fragment of camouflage parachute fabric and regaled us with stories of his wartime exploits. Tom could pronounce his name – Monsieur Leroux – and remembers it still and, initially, French was to become one of his favourite subjects in his new unit.

Very early in the first week of senior school Tom lost his heart to a hearing girl in his tutor group. When she threw a pencil in class it grazed his eye and I had to take him to the doctor, who said serious damage would have been caused had it been just a millimetre out. Manfully protecting the object of his new devotion, Tom concocted a quite different story from the one that eventually emerged and for a time we really did believe it was a big bully boy in the playground who was the cause of what could have been a disastrous accident for someone so doubly dependent on his eyesight!

Forging an instant bond at Tom's first meeting with John Barry

. . . and a friendship that has flourished over the years

Just as Tom was coping with the challenge of a new school, a 'For sale' board appeared at the house opposite where his great friend Caroline lived. Right out of the blue the family was emigrating to Australia. Breaking the news to a devastated Tom was like announcing an impending death and I just hated having to do it. He didn't cry until he went upstairs to confide in Daniel. Afterwards he told me he was imagining Caroline doing things in Australia and, a week or so later when he was considering the possibility of other children moving into her house, he decided, 'I will not make friends with them because I have to do my homework. I don't want them coming ringing the bell – "can Thomas come out to play?" – because I have homework'. I think he was somehow reconciling himself to the idea, trying to see it as a positive thing that would give him more time for his school work and, at the same time, protecting himself by erecting barriers against any new youngsters who may prove less accommodating than Caroline. Trying to be positive myself I wondered if a world-wide separation might not in the long run be better than her simply outgrowing him, which might well have happened as the inevitable language gulf between them widened. Now in her twenties she is back living locally and they are good friends again, especially since she knows he can still be relied upon to go to fun places like Alton Towers Adventure Theme Park, ice skating and other outdoor pursuits involving just an element of risk!

When a younger, hearing friend, Josh, came to play with him on the computer 11-year-old Tom produced some games for which he had written out pages of concise, detailed instructions since he knew he couldn't explain them verbally. Josh's mum, Celia, a friend I'd made at the Toddler Group I ran, was a social worker with deaf people and seemed amazed that a boy as deaf as Tom should have such command of clear, written language. Her partner, John, a profoundly deaf man, declared himself proud that I could sign. He was to prove a good role model in many ways and he and Tom got on famously from the start. It was good to see them years later working together on the Bromley Chain committee and on that of the much-needed Bromley Deaf Social Club they themselves helped to set up in the year 2000 and for which Tom is the Treasurer. And this friendship might never have come about had I not questioned the yellow sticker 'Mind that child might be deaf' that I spotted in Celia's rear window in the church hall car park.

Video Memories

Despite the rigours of the National Curriculum, some extra-mural activities took place with the unit, one being the visit to the Mayor's Parlour in Bromley where the deaf students tried on the mayoral robes and handled

Delusions of grandeur at the Mayor's Parlour

the regalia as they were given an insight into civic ceremonies. Like me, Jackie and her splendid team were firm believers in snapping or videoing every event in order to extract the maximum mileage out of every photo opportunity.

The use of the video in curriculum work was also to prove beneficial when Jackie devised her own original Video Memory project. Tom loved this, not least because throughout her submission to the *Journal of the British Association of Teachers of the Deaf* ('Memory – The forgotten cognitive skill: Encouraging the development of memory strategies in signing pupils' which appeared in their issue dated September 1996 Vol. 20, No. 4, pp. 101–10) for reasons of anonymity she referred to him as 'Todd', his favourite character in the Australian 'Neighbours' soap at that time! (K, his Indian peer had changed her first name on entry to senior school, in keeping with her cultural tradition, and Tom was obsessively jealous of her ability to do this and couldn't understand why he couldn't change his Christian name to Todd.) Jackie used her project to improve the memory skills of profoundly deaf pupils whose preferred means of communication was through SSE. The aim was to transfer the oral / aural principles used with Dr Colin Lane's multi-sensory ARROW (Aural-Read-Respond-Oral-Written) tape recording technique (where children with useful residual hearing learn by listening to their own voices) for a visual medium.

Jackie's pilot study was started in Year 7 with Tom and K and material from their science lessons from the main school formed the basis for the new type of memory work. By Year 10 its worth had been proved when both were at the top of their set with scores of 20% to 30% above the average, whereas in Year 7 both had been average or slightly below. During that period the videos had enabled both families to share in the learning process too and I particularly appreciated the opportunity to be a 'fly on the wall' at school. Tom would fingerspell, sign and speak to consolidate the new concepts and it was, it seemed, important to both pupils that they used their own voices on the videos. Jackie wondered if that was because of the 'imperialism of a hearing culture' or whether they simply wanted to receive the optimum information. They were, apparently, dismayed when, on one particularly bright and sunny day, their hands were clearly visible but they could not see their faces on screen.

More Commitments

Although within school I could see the gap widening between Tom and his main-school peers, he continued his involvement with the Deaf Drama Club in London and with local hearing friends, and various day and night hikes took place with the 6th Beckenham South Scouts which he had joined, insisting on using his voice, rather than signs, for the Promise. Also at St George's, in May 1992 he attended, with seven others, his first Confirmation class, run by lay reader, Steffen Conway. I went along to sign for Tom and during the year-long course he compiled a beautiful book of worksheets. Meanwhile his poor RE results in his summer exams at school did not endear him to his tutor who would, I think, have liked to have had him excommunicated even before the event when he wrote 'Jesus was the founder of Islam' and 'I forget what plagueses [sic] is!' However, Tom *was* confirmed by the Bishop of Tonbridge in November 1992, in St Paul's Church, Beckenham, and to our delight both Jackie Parsons and John Hurd accompanied us, together with his godfather, Paul, and his family. Tom's clear, emphatic 'Amen' as he stepped back from the Bishop made us all gasp – and made me reach hastily for a tissue.

As well as an Elisabeth Leishman Bavarian wax candle with praying hands and bearing his name and the date, I also gave Tom a prayer book compiled by David Silk, the priest who had been Rector of St George's during his babyhood. I wrote in it

> Thomas, I am giving you this on your Confirmation Day because it was David Silk who *blessed* you when you were two weeks old, *baptised* you

Tom took his investiture at Scouts very seriously

when you were three months old, *anointed* you when you were five months old (in hospital). God heard my prayers then and He will always hear you . . . 25.11.1992.

Two years later David himself inscribed the prayer book when he visited Beckenham just prior to being consecrated as Bishop of Ballarat, Australia, at Westminster Abbey. He told me Tom's was a story he would never forget and has now done us the honour of writing the Introduction.

Late in the summer of 1992, after much deliberation (and with some trepidation on my part) the local consultant paediatrician decided to start decreasing the medication for his epilepsy. It just so happened that at that time the unit's special support assistant was having a major operation and Jackie asked me if I would be prepared to work a few weeks to cover her convalescence. It seemed a good idea as my signing skills and deaf awareness would be useful and, although I would not be working with him, I would be on hand should anything unforeseen happen to Tom. Fortunately all was well and it was particularly gratifying when Tom's tutor found a big improvement in his work, especially in maths, once the carbamazapine was phased out gradually, over a period of six months. It felt almost too good to be true that the three-year span of dependence on drugs was coming to a close, although it was to be a while before we could really relax completely and an emergency treatment was always on hand in case of an unexpected seizure. But, knowing his yearning to drive, I was hugely relieved to feel that Tom might, after all, be able to do so at the appropriate time. The thought that he might be denied this opportunity was one of the things that had grieved me immediately the diagnosis of epilepsy had been made. So shattering to visualise him growing up, still deaf but not, as promised in the bath that night long years before, allowed to drive a car. The likely loss of that privilege had felt very hard to me.

Scouts was an activity Tom continued to enjoy and I think the attitudes, activities and confidence he learnt with them stood him in good stead later when he moved on to bigger challenges. He wrote in his school self awareness book 'I like going to Scouts because I could learn to do things that I could help other people' and said, when he had done a sponsored swim in Crystal Palace's Olympic pool for the British Heart Foundation in 1993 and told me that his legs had 'run out of energy', that he did things like that 'because I am a Scout, I am a Christian and I care about people'. And what, he was asked in Year 9, would he like to change about himself. 'I might want to hear more and I want to be good at everything'.

His annual statement review at school read that he was now travelling independently, on public transport, and was 'an absolute delight to teach – quick to follow, intelligent, has a wicked sense of humour'.

Thanks to inspiring teachers, he appeared to excel at English and Drama. In the Year 9 summer examinations he amazed us all by coming top of the main-school mixed ability drama class with 91%. He had loved the work on 'Midsummer Night's Dream' and, because of his exposure to the Deaf Drama Club in London, where he had the chance to work not only with Sarah Scott and Ray Harrison Graham but also with the late poet Dot Miles, actress Paula Garfield, David Bowers (later to find fame in 'Four Weddings and a Funeral'), John Wilson, now of SHAPE Arts and Antony Rabin, he had plenty to offer in the way of ideas. He was also able to constructively appraise his own and others' work when it came to the written part of the test.

In 1994 the unit's special support assistant, whose convalescence I had covered, retired and, since funding did not allow for her to be replaced by a teacher of the deaf, as they had hoped, Jackie asked me if I would consider applying for the post. I did so reluctantly, having first asked Tom how *he* would feel about it. There was no real objection from him and, since I would be entering *his* territory if I was appointed, rather than the other way round, I felt reasonably comfortable about the idea. In April I started as an SSA,

Carrying the flag at the St. George's Day parade

working with different pupils in different subjects but, for obvious reasons, never with Tom's group. He himself was growing so fast that I would occasionally not recognise him when I saw him in the distance across a sea of teenagers. To spare his feelings it was *de rigueur* to ignore each other if we travelled on the same bus – but on more than one occasion he was kind enough to give me a surreptitious nudge as he got off with his friends and could see I was so sound asleep I'd be likely to miss the next stop!

When his brother Daniel left home to start a BA Honours degree course in graphic design at Brighton, Tom and I treated ourselves to a signed performance of 'Starlight Express' to cheer us up the evening following his departure. We all missed him terribly but Tom probably most of all for, as he explained in a letter to his godfather, 'I am still bored to death without Dan around!'

The fact that Dan was no longer available to help out at Scouts didn't mean Tom gave up his commitment. He became a patrol leader and was given the honour of carrying the Union Jack at the big St George's Day parade in 1995, leading the hundreds of Rainbows, Cubs, Scouts and Venture Scouts in and out of a packed St George's Church, and causing me to recall how he had first gone to such an event at the age of three years when his two Cub brothers were taking part and how, after I'd removed him when he became restless, a fascinated stranger in the congregation had later told me outside that it was not nearly such fun after we'd left!

In order that he didn't miss out because his was such a small troop he was invited to join with the one from West Wickham Methodist Church for a five-day camp and went off, full of confidence, with a group of hearing boys unknown to him. He loved it and wrote to thank the scoutmaster on his return:

> *Dear Stuart,*
> *I would like to write to you to say how much I enjoyed the camp with your boys. It was such a successful camp and I had an absolutely fabulous time. I really appreciate your offer to me to camp with your troop.*
>
> *I have had such a great time. Could you please say thank you to everybody who helped me to understand, it was no problem. Also could you tell everyone that I had good fun being with you all and I had great time camping with you.*
>
> *I liked seeing your children at the camp, they are really cute and I think you have got a lovely family.*
>
> *I hope to meet you all again, Yours, Thomas.*

Making Friends, Influencing People

The charity Friends for Young Deaf People (FYD) are committed to a total communication policy and recognise the importance of all the different methods of communication, including BSL, SSE, use of the voice and lip-reading. Their deaf and hearing partnership is open to everyone which is why their annual sports day (when youngsters were able to sample a huge variety of different sports and activities with qualified coaches, supervisors and communicators) at the nearby Crystal Palace Sports Centre had been a highlight of Tom's holidays since he was six years old. Now 15 he felt ready to broaden his horizons and, in the summer

Making new friends at FYD's Bude Challenge 1995

holidays, to take up their Bude Challenge, run by Adventure International, in Cornwall. He went without knowing anyone and was very apprehensive beforehand, despite the assured ease of communication, but the promise of outdoor activities – sailing, abseiling, swimming, surfing, canoeing, windsurfing, orienteering and assault course – appealed to him greatly. He was in the winning team and returned home absolutely elated and with new friends and a new-found confidence. As a result he couldn't wait for the following summer when, yet again, his was the winning team.

The involvement with FYD led to him going on to their Initiative Training Course weekends, where he learnt about teamwork in the company of deaf, hard of hearing and hearing people, thanks to that excellent ethos where all forms of communication are embraced. When he went to Bude for the third year running, in 1997, he was in a different role, going as part of his Post Initiative Training and came home with the casual query, 'Did you see anything about us on the News?' It transpired that the first aid and lifesaving skills employed on the beach had been so realistic that the Air / Sea Rescue Service had been summoned and the course leader reprimanded for not alerting coastguards before holidaymakers took it as a genuine emergency! The course also included raft making and survival techniques, working in teams, and this time Tom came home with a distinction.

Next on the FYD agenda was their excellent Action Centred Development workshops which took place in different parts of the country and

Awarded the Laurie Davies Cup for progress by
a Deaf Pupil 1995

gave Tom the chance to mix with other deaf and hearing youngsters as they
learnt together about counselling, advocacy, assertiveness, stress management and empowerment. As a practical part of his commitment to the
course he had to help plan a Caribbean party at a deaf club on the far side of
London and he gave up two consecutive Easter holidays to be a volunteer
supervisor at the FYD family weekends at Charterhouse, Surrey, and also
supervised at some sports days.

In what was to be Tom's final academic year at Darrick Wood School he
was awarded the Laurie Davies cup for progress by a deaf pupil; it seemed
a good start to an eventful six months. In the autumn the Year 11 work
experience commenced and Tom spent a week in an Orpington printing
company. Declaring, 'I'm not ready for this' he was very worried beforehand but was made to feel so welcome and was so happy that he soon lost

any qualms. The firm's appraisal for school reported 'excellent in all areas, worked extremely hard and showed great initiative'.

This experience formed part of the special school leavers' programme which the deaf students followed in the Hearing Impairment Unit. It was a comprehensive and excellent course devised by Lynne, a teacher of the deaf, who took them to the Houses of Parliament, introduced them to the complexities of local government, health issues, relationships, self-aware-ness, the world of work, communication issues and suchlike and provided a lively and thought-provoking forum where all their concerns and capa-bilities could be discussed. As with everything in the HIU, in particular maths and English, much work was done in small groups, so that the deaf students had time to consolidate information from main-school lessons or learn specific things at their own pace and with their own special needs suitably addressed. This seemed to me to give them the best of both worlds – integration and differentiation – rather than the segregation of being away from home in a boarding school for deaf youngsters. Some adult deaf friends have admitted to me that after that experience the outside, hearing world all too often comes as something of a rude awakening.

Reaping the reward of all the early signing and watching, in speech hearing tests towards the end of his schooling Tom's score, with Signed English and lip-reading, was 92%; with lip-reading alone it was 72%. His teachers were pleased with these results and Jackie had been impressed with his enthusiasm and commitment in the work she had done with him. 'I have counted it a privilege to teach Tom and see him mature into a fine young man with a ready sense of humour and sensitivity to the feelings and needs of others', she wrote. We could ask for no better testimonial, from no finer a teacher of the deaf, than that!

In the autumn half term Tom and two of his deaf friends travelled up to Doncaster College for the Deaf Careers Convention to do some tests and see what was on offer there. In his English assessment Tom got 96%, and in maths 74%. They commented that he 'made every effort to supply informa-tion and be helpful. It was not an easy task but Thomas really tried to overcome his shyness'. Each of these 'challenges' in 1995 were small but significant steps for a student whose earlier abundant confidence seemed to be fast deserting him in certain situations.

For reasons which will become apparent in the following chapters, 1996 was to be a very momentous year for Tom and not only because of the GCSEs, the results of which disappointed him. He had Ds for maths, English Literature, English Language (with a B for coursework) and geography, and Es for double science and design & technology/food. He had so hoped for a C in geography but we were acutely aware that in the

A winning wave from the Crystal Palace
podium, 1996

period prior to the examinations he had undergone two long anaesthetics
and had been through a potentially stressful experience. In between
leaving Scouts in January and school in May, a major event in his life had
taken place.

Luckily, there were also lighter moments. Thanks to the fact that, out of
33 London boroughs competing in the Heathrow Youth Games – London
1996 at Crystal Palace National Sports Centre, only two could produce deaf
boys under 17 years to run in the 200 metres, Tom found himself on the very
same podium that had held one of his heroes, Linford Christie, only two
days previously. He won the gold medal but I think he would have felt
more elated about it if the other contestant hadn't had additional difficulties and if he himself had faced stiff competition! Nevertheless, he had run
so fast that his father didn't recognise him when he covered the distance in
27.9 seconds and his marks helped the borough to their final, respectable,
place.

New Directions

In the autumn of 1996, together with three peers who had been his
companions since nursery days in the unit and with excellent signing/

note-taking support from City Lit, London, Tom commenced at Croydon College in Surrey on the GNVQ Intermediate Information Technology course. In his spare time he volunteered to help paint scenery for the St George's Players, where the rector, impressed by his concentration and application to the task in hand, noted that he didn't lark about like the other youngsters were wont to do. What *he* saw as an asset I'm afraid *I* regarded as a sad reflection on Tom's lack of hearing. Yet again he was missing out on the incidental fun in which other teenagers can revel. Still undaunted, Tom became a helper in Junior Church and volunteered with a hearing friend from his Confirmation days to help edit and layout *Dragonfly*, a free news-sheet for church youngsters, as well as helping me produce *Chainmail*, the twice yearly Bromley Chain newsletter. He enjoyed writing articles for it and, unlike the few other contributors, never had to be chased for copy. I like to think some of my old friends from *Woman's Weekly* days might say it's in the genes!

Many changes were afoot in other areas of our lives. In June 1997 Daniel graduated from Brighton with a 2.1 degree in graphic design and Tom was awarded distinction in his college course, equivalent to several high GCSE grades. Jackie had already left the unit and in July John Hurd, who had been such a support ever since that first visit to the baby Tom and who had foresightedly employed her very much with him and his peers in mind, retired as Head of Sensory Support Services. It was definitely the end of another era. In a thank you letter after the few brief words I had found the courage to stand up and say at his leaving party, John wrote:

> You have been the reason for Tom's development – intellectually and as a person. That you associate me with that achievement is embarrass-ing and undeserved . . . If only more people could enjoy their kids instead of looking at them as specimens for discussion and therapy, there'd be more happy deaf people.

Wise words from a wise man and coming, as it did, at a very fragile time in the autumn term, that letter meant a lot to me.

The day before I returned to school for what was to be my last and least happy term there, Princess Diana died. Tom was very sad and shocked and, because of his own similarity in age, I am sure he must have identified with the feelings of the two young princes at that time. He himself was just about to enrol at the London College of Printing on their digital origination course which incorporated all the Mac programmes which his father used in the printing company. He spent two days a week at college and the remainder of the time was working with John, in Dartford. Whilst attending the LCP, where he obtained a Merit pass in his BTEC course, Tom was on the student forum of the London Institute.

Widening his experiences still further, he passed CACDP Stage One BSL and joined the committee of Bromley Chain, the local charity launched in the year of his birth, becoming a second generation member who, having benefited over the years from its play schemes, parties, equipment provision, signed pantomimes and suchlike, was willing to play his part in keeping it going.

Driving Ambition

Once Tom had started full-time work at Froude Printing, officially as a trainee Mac Operator but also doing other things such as print finishing, dark room work, and so on, he wanted to learn to drive. He and Dan had bought a little red Mini between them, which Tom had promptly named 'Red October' since, after much hunting, that was the month they finally found it in 1997. Much to his disappointment, however, he couldn't hear the engine to know when to change the gears, despite fitting a rev counter, and wasn't confident enough to drive on the highway.

Driving itself may have been put in abeyance but he decided to do his theory test. After two frustrating attempts when he missed a pass by just one mark each time, he went (with me signing and note-taking for him) to a day-long seminar at the local civic centre and I think this intensive input must have helped since, shortly after, the day before his nineteenth birthday, he took the test again and passed with 35/35. I think he paid the additional fee as a birthday present to himself, so that he would be given the results immediately. I was all too aware it could make or mar his birthday but what a joyous fax that was to receive via the Nokia Communicator mobile phone we had given him for his eighteenth birthday!

Frustrated as he was with his lack of physical driving skills, Tom decided to invest his time, money and energy in something he knew he could manage well. Knowing what technophobes his parents are he wrote us a long letter a few months before his nineteenth birthday, explaining what he had in mind.

Dear Mum and Dad,

I don't know how to start this – it's all about joining Internet, you know I'm into these stuff with computers. Sorry I kept avoiding to speak to you about connecting Internet.

I've always known that you will give same answer to each time I ask this sort of question and I wonder if you will have the change of heart this time?

I would like you to consider about getting our computer hooked on Internet as you know that I'm 18 and I'm willing to pay for on-line phone bills and membership fee. I've bought this subject up again because I think I've found cheapest Internet service and thought it was good deal, it is not top brand

Internet service like AOL, it is quite new service called Free.dot.net at £40 for 2 years or £75 for 5 years with e-mail at 99p per week plus around £2.20 per hour on-line.

I still do not know how much do you really know about Internet(?) You don't need to understand the technology – think of the benefit we could gain from Internet, refer to 'Computers don't bite' magazine if you need to know more.

I feel confident that I can afford the on-line costs if I can promise you that I will watch my time on Internet.

I've come to my decision that I will sell the Mini to Dan but I still do not have the guts to break this news to him. Also I decided to quit driving for while.

Of course Internet won't be always be for me to surf – you still can use it if you want me to teach you and see what you have been missing out.

Internet have endless info – miss anything important? Internet always have the information (e.g. missed your favourite programme).

As you can see we are often busy or tired. I won't be spending long time surfing but I can use it in weekends – for while in weekdays.

I will take my own responsibilities for all of these and pay for it and I know what I'm doing. I can get a modem for about £80 (if you need 'Computers don't bite' mag it is in my room).

Internet is probably the last thing on your mind but I wanted to check with you then you can leave it to me. With love, Tom.

After a letter like that – embodying sales talk, gentle persuasion, a polite understanding of our technical ignorance, an awareness of costs and a good bit of research – yes, of course, he got his access to the Internet!

It was a lucky day when Dan was given an old automatic car to dispose of for a friend who'd gone abroad. Tom gave it a trial. 'Magic' he declared when he got home, 'it's so easy!' A series of driving lessons in an automatic car were booked with an instructor found via the Mobility Centre at Sutton, Surrey and it was indeed magical to see Tom's confidence blossom after so much despondency. After the first two sessions I asked him why he was so loath to take a block booking of ten lessons which would work out cheaper. 'I may only need five' he mused, until I pointed out in no uncertain terms that that number may be fine for someone with access to a car for evening/weekend practising but not for someone dependent on lessons alone. Fairly furious with me he did reluctantly agree to a final total of 15 lessons, plus two practices with a dear interpreter friend from Bromley Chain who was brave enough to sit with him in her automatic.

On his application form for a driving test Tom had indicated his need for an interpreter and we had assumed one would be booked automatically as had happened for the theory tests. However when he faxed with the wonderful news that he had passed at the first attempt ('I am still shaking') he made no mention of it, and it was only later that he told his brother no interpreter had appeared. We were doubly delighted that he'd coped with lip-reading alone, since it would have been easy for Dan to accompany him had we known, as I later discovered from the Driving Standards Agency, that it is up to the would-be driver to make his/her own interpreter arrangements for the practical test. Pleased with his prowess, Tom promptly bought himself a second-hand Golf, making all the necessary arrangements and coping with the paperwork by himself, and has proved a confident and careful driver, proud to give his useless mother a lift but very aware of my body language on the first few journeys.

'Don't you trust my driving?' he demanded. My 'baby' had well and truly grown up!

Chapter 8

Sound or Silence?

Silence is deep as eternity, noise shallow as time. (Thomas Carlyle)

A chance remark led us on a journey that was to take many years and, hopefully, will have no end. Tom, aged 13, was asking me about different forms of deaf education. Reminding him of his old friend Daniel who, after moving to Sussex, was in a school for the deaf rather than a unit, I searched for some ways of identifying him quickly.

'You remember, he lives in Brighton, and he had a cochlear implant'. Tom nodded, thought for a minute or two, and then said with great feeling 'I wish I was him'.

'Why, because he lives at the seaside?' I queried, thinking immediately of the attractions of the beach. 'No', came the scornful reply, 'because of the implant!'

I was momentarily stunned but asked him if he would like to be considered for one. In typically quaint fashion he answered, 'It would be my pleasure!'

Of course, we knew about cochlear implants. Thanks to media hype even many people who have no conception of what deafness actually means, let alone what its implications are for a youngster, have heard of them and numerous were the newspaper cuttings sent to me over the years from friends or relatives who had read an article hailing the 'miracle bionic ear' and its attendant sensational success story.

At that first visit to an ENT consultant immediately following the meningitis, he had told us categorically that Thomas would go on a list and would receive one when he was ten. Just like that! No explanation as to what it meant, what an implant entailed or, more importantly, how we coped in the meantime. It was only when that same person explained, somewhat defensively, that the six-month delay between diagnosis of deafness and our being sent to the appropriate specialist centre for Tom to receive hearing aids was 'neither here nor there at this age' that I realised he himself was no expert in the management of profoundly deaf infants. I felt stupidly gullible (and not for the first time!) when I realised it was 'pie in

Listening and speaking work had always played
a big part in the HIU

the sky' but at least by then we had support from people who had become
special and strategies to use which gave us the confidence to cope. I was
sorely tempted, however, to arrive on the consultant's doorstep with Tom
on his tenth birthday and demand the promised implant then and there!

Over those early years I did acquire more information about cochlear
implants. In 1990 I went to a parents' talk in Woolwich given by Philip
Evans, an audiological scientist at Guy's Hospital, and Carlo Laurenzi of
the National Deaf Children's Society (NDCS) where the implant was put
into perspective and described, not as a 'miracle cure' but as 'simply a
sophisticated hearing aid'. I knew Tom had nerve deafness due to the
meningitis so when I heard references to an implant stimulating the
auditory nerve I assumed his was now defunct and he would not,
therefore, be a suitable candidate even if we wanted one. In fact, of course, it
is the nerves in the little hairs in the cochlea itself which are damaged but, in
any event, in the early 1980s the NDCS had been so against the use of
implants with young children that, having read their rationale and
attended a talk by Harry Cayton, then their director, when Tom was a
toddler, I was convinced they were not the answer for him.

However, things move on and technology improves all the time. Tom had
received such negligible input from his hearing aids and was, as a result, so
laid back about their use and often so unaware when the batteries were flat
that I really felt he was not interested in hearing. It was not until we trans-

ferred from the Nuffield Centre to Guy's Hospital in March 1991 where, a year later, he was at last allowed the powerful Phonak Super PPCL 4+ aids which I had been requesting ever since the Woolwich talk, that at the age of 12 he finally derived some benefit. Maybe this made him feel greedy for more sound. The consultant at Guy's had suggested at one of our first visits that possibly a cochlear implant would be the only thing which would really help and that he might be considered as a potential candidate in the future. As at that time Tom was on medication for epilepsy and there was no way I wanted to jeopardise that situation with a general anaesthetic, invasive surgery and electrical stimulation near the brain, or even just the stress of an assessment, I had mentally put the whole subject on hold.

By the time Tom made his own request, the fairly brief period of epilepsy appeared to be over and the drugs were gradually being withdrawn. We felt he had done so well for so long with next to nothing in the way of useful amplification that, if an implant was allowed, it would be a bonus he richly deserved if it helped him to be aware of environmental sounds and of people talking to him, so that his already excellent lip-reading could improve. For safety and for socialising, for feeling more a part of the world, we felt it would be a huge help, but only because he himself wanted it. In October 1993 an 'improved auditory discrimination' was noted and the consultant felt we should give the Phonak aids a slightly longer trial, to which we reluctantly agreed.

Two months later I attended a cochlear implant seminar run by Great Ormond Street Children's Hospital (GOSH) during which I felt hopeful, from what was said, that Tom's own motivation and level of language would be in his favour. During the presentations it also became apparent that there could be a considerable delay between referral and assessment. In view of this, I duly requested the wheels be set in motion earlier but even so it was September 1994 before our GP's fund-holding practice wrote to say they would pay for the initial assessment at GOSH, since Guy's own cochlear implant programme was not yet in existence.

To our delight, in January 1995 things started moving and we felt we were getting somewhere at long last. The cochlear implant team sent us forms and questionnaires for the Hearing Impairment Unit to fill in. Jackie Parsons endorsed Tom's application with a letter in which she described his grasp of language as 'absolutely unshakeable', continuing

> the excellent foundations laid at home and in the Primary Unit have stood him in really good stead for the whole of the curriculum. Thomas continues to have full and enthusiastic support from home and has discussed the implications of an implant at great length. He has a realistic idea of both the benefits and the limitations of such an operation and is

as concerned about how his mother would feel if he had an implant, as he is about his own response to it.

Sudden Setback

We were on the verge of receiving an appointment at GOSH when everything ground to a distressing and totally unexpected halt. Bromley Health refused to allow the assessment to take place, partly because in its first year as an NHS Trust the hospital was not allowed to accept the funding offered, and because, had Tom been deemed a suitable recipient, the operation would need to be carried out within a set period of time under government guidelines, something that could not be guaranteed financially. It also transpired that the referral, coming as it did from a consultant audiological scientist rather than a medical consultant, carried less weight. This was hard to accept, since his assessment and management of Tom's hearing loss had been the best we had received in 14 years of deafness.

With Tom growing daily more despondent and public exams looming on the horizon we felt we needed to know as a matter of urgency if he was likely to be a suitable candidate, and be able to make plans accordingly. To me, it seemed essential that any implant should take place when he was still at school, with the psychological and professional support of friends and teachers available. This set-back, then, was the start of the most frustrating period but one which, true to form, Tom turned to good advantage since he used the experience to research implants, to make a case for teenagers to receive them and for more funding to be available. Initially I contented myself by covering a ring binder file with spare, collaged photographs of him, from babyhood to the current time, simply to cheer myself up with happy, uncomplicated memories of this beloved son of ours. The file soon bulged as I filled it with copies of the countless letters I wrote, challenging the whole, very strange, situation.

The consultant at Guy's agreed that my concern about the effect of the delay upon Thomas and his education was 'entirely valid'. I wrote to Lord Ashley who in turn contacted a consultant on the University College London (UCL) Adult Cochlear Implant Programme, who felt the refusal for referral was based on financial grounds. I then wrote to Robert Newton at the NHS Management Executive, who stated that financial grounds should not be a reason for refusing extra contractual referrals. I also contacted Virginia Bottomley as Health Secretary, our own MP Piers Merchant and, of course, wrote numerous letters to Bromley Health.

Tom, meanwhile, was conducting his own research and using it for a presentation as part of his GCSE English coursework (for which he gained a B grade). Thanks to Tricia Kemp of the Cochlear Implant Children's

Support Group, a personal friend since her young son Alex was at that time attending Darrick Wood Primary Unit, we discovered that Piers Kittel (of similar age and communication background to Tom) had received an implant at the age of 14. I so well remembered seeing him signing on the BBC television programme 'See Hear' at about the age of three and thinking then how like Tom he was in his confidence and communication.

We were fascinated to read Piers's and his parents' accounts of the pre- and post-operative events, their fears, hopes and feelings with regard to themselves, the school and the Deaf community, contained in a Workshop Report March 1995 – 'Cochlear implant and bilingualism'. That same month Tom wrote to Piers, sending him a questionnaire for his English project and ended his letter 'I am fed up waiting for cochlear implant. I may not get it. I envy you'. We digested both the BDA viewpoint contained in their 'Policy on cochlear implants'(1994) making a strong case against them for children, and the NDCS ones, 'Cochlear implants' (1990) and 'Cochlear implants and deaf children' (1994), which I felt were very much more balanced, helpful and impartial.

Some Deaf acquaintances were convinced an implant would be to the detriment of Tom's personality. Another friend, a hearing aid user with an oral upbringing but now part of the Deaf community, made it clear that she was against them. But when she was able to respond to footsteps outside the classroom and queried 'Who was that?' I was quite aggrieved at her stance. I felt Tom was justified in wanting sound for himself that would tell him someone was around. If and when he marries it will more than likely be to a deaf person but it does not follow that any offspring will be deaf. He owes it to them to be able to have some hearing and the sort of confidence and language that does not make him reliant on them or on social workers for everything. I have met deaf teenagers who, surprisingly enough, appear anything but proud of their deaf parents' lifestyles and I have also met deaf parents who have reacted with fury to the suggestion that their new-born baby might be deaf. Deaf pride is not always as evident as some in its community would like to think.

In the spring of 1995 our then MP, Piers Merchant, sent me a copy of a letter he had received from the Chief Executive of Bromley Health, confessing that cochlear implants presented them with a 'series of difficult challenges'. I pointed out that to suffer from profound deafness is to face a *lifetime* of difficult challenges!

Assessment Begins

As the new financial year dawned, a different system with funding came into being and on 11 May 1995 Tom was approved as a priority for an implant. Bromley Health had identified the candidates – 'a maximum of two' – for the year and he was one of them. Those five frustrating months had felt like five years but in June we had our long-awaited appointment with the late Dr. Sue Bellman at GOSH. We were elated!

She pulled no punches. She was at pains to explain that they were not assessing Thomas to see if *he* was suitable for the implant, but to see if the implant was suitable for *him*. She wondered what sound meant to him and what use he made of it? That made me worry whether those six months after the meningitis and before the aids had been obtained would have been vital in stimulating his residual hearing. Had he lost *more* because of the infuriating delay?

Dr Bellman emphasised that he had been deaf for so long the implant couldn't give him all he would wish. Tom made his feelings clear. 'I am not expecting to hear speech'. As we sat there, in a department geared to tiny children, I felt Dr Bellman thought him too old to benefit although she seemed impressed with his lip-reading and the integration aspect of school. She showed him photographs of the sort of scar he could expect and talked about the risk of damage to the facial nerve which could result in *permanent* facial paralysis. He was visibly shaken by this and she gave him ten days in which to ponder on it and the other aspects she had raised. I think she recognised in him a teenager who would take these factors on board and she was happy to see him obviously preparing to consider them very seriously. I, in turn, had my own doubts. A possible return of the epilepsy still haunted me and I also thought of the rise in street crime and the implications of a desperately vulnerable head in the hands of a mugger.

On the way out of the hospital we visited the League of Friends' shop and bought a card depicting an elephant with miles of audio tape emerging from each huge ear. 'Long time no hear' was its simple message. And what could have been more apt than that?

Once home Tom gave more thought to the risks and admitted his fears to me, 'If so many young children have had a cochlear implant and have survived perhaps when it's my turn I will not be lucky'. But after family discussions he made up his mind to go ahead with the assessment and in July had a CT scan in order to check that the meningitis had not left so much ossification in the cochlea that it would be impossible to insert the electrodes; fortunately the scan was normal. He had several sessions with Kelly, an audiologist and Clare, a speech therapist. He wrote to a hearing friend from church about the brain stem response test which, as far as he was concerned, was the only unpleasant part of the assessment procedure.

Dear Elanor,

I thought I would write to you to tell you my latest news on Cochlear Implant assessment I have had.

You know I went to Great Ormond Street hospital for CT scan some time ago; the CT scan showed that my ear was clear and normal and I was allowed to carry on going to hospital for more tests. If my ear wasn't clear I would have to stop visiting the hospital because there is no possibility for cochlear implant.

On 30th August I went to G.O.S.H. for 2 tests. My first test was really painful but I was really alright. My Audiological Scientist, Kelly, put some stuff which contains sand in it and had to be rubbed on behind both my ears real hard to get rid of oily skin, and I couldn't stand the pain. I suppose it sounds sickening. A wire was attached behind my ears and I had to lie down to sleep for a little time and I get results from computer to see how my brain respond to sound.

Areas behind my ears were so painful and it was so dry and left red marks for a day then became a scab.

The 2nd tests was speech and language. It was real easy, simple. I had only to say a word for e.g. 'car', 'gate', 'cat'. I was being filmed; these tests show how well I say a word. Also the speech therapist will ask me some questions and I have to find the right picture e.g. there is 3 pictures (1) girl running (2) girl jumping (3) boy running. I got to point out which I think the therapist said without signing, lip-read only. Next piece, some listening work. I will be visiting G.O.S.H. again soon.

If the hospital thinks that I am suitable for cochlear implant, the operation would be in January 1996 next year. I have got few more tests to go then It should be over.

I hope this letter didn't bore you. See you tonight if you are coming to Youth Club. We are having B.B.Q.

See ya, from a friend, Thomas.

In September, during a speech therapy session, Clare emphasised that were it not for Tom's good language and lip-reading skills she would not recommend him for an implant. He was simply too old for all the work that would need to be done beforehand. She felt it was excellent that he could discuss the pros and cons of the operation and the team could feel that he was really listening to their viewpoints. She had expected him to get discouraged with all the tests but he had kept going.

The following month, we were told, a team of 17 people would discuss Tom's case. Kelly, meanwhile, did some Manchester Tests, in which he scored 10 out of 12 – 'magnificent!' She was really impressed and tremendously happy with him but she told us she had to point out that his age may be against him. When she said this Tom and I both noticed that she had tears in her eyes. 'Did you see . . . ?' he asked me on the train going home afterwards.

We received the initial assessment report from Mary, an implant team teacher of the deaf, in September. In it he was referred to as 'mature, sensible and realistic in his expectations'. In tests of his speech perception and lip-reading at school in an unseen passage of dictation with lip-reading and sign he had scored 98%, with lip-reading alone he scored 68%. She felt he was a good candidate for implantation.

Her telephone call on 12 October told me he had been selected, partly because of his 'positive attitude'. I hadn't expected I would cry quite so much when I put the phone down . . .

The following Sunday we sang one of my favourite hymns, number 52 in the English Hymnal, in church. We had already had our 'mornings of joy' which had been given for those devastating 'evenings of tearfulness' all those years ago in Farnborough Hospital, and then 'Trust for our trembling and hope for our fear' following diagnosis of deafness. But now we needed help again in the hope that we were all making the right decision. 'Low at his feet lay thy burden of carefulness, High on his heart he will bear it for thee; Comfort thy sorrows and answer thy prayerfulness, Guiding thy steps as may best for thee be'. Once again I knew we were in good hands.

A week later the official confirmation letter was received and on the day Tom and I went in half term to meet Piers and his parents, he posted his acceptance of the offer. It was interesting to me to note that he carefully popped it into the letter box before we caught the train to Hertfordshire, obviously already so clear in his own mind that this was the right course of action for him. And, having met Piers, there were no second thoughts – just happy anticipation and, naturally, some trepidation, too.

Although Tom's operation was scheduled for January, in December it looked as if an earlier opportunity would be offered, when it seemed that other parents wavering in their decision might well choose not to go ahead at that time. For a whole day we were on tenterhooks. Would it really have been right to take Tom straight after his geography mock GCSE and admit him to hospital? On the other hand, if this chance was offered and declined and then, come January, he had a cold or cough and had to cancel, we would be getting ever nearer to the public exams and all that they entailed. It was a tricky situation but, fortunately, one which was resolved when the other family eventually decided to go ahead as planned. A relief, of course, for us but I also felt pleased that their dilemma had been resolved.

On Christmas day Thomas wrote a letter for his family.

Hands that sign can also be used as a haven for a
cherished hamster!

Dear Mum, Dad, Matthew and Daniel,
As you see I am 15 years old and I am really hopeless at Christmas shopping
and I have had some difficulty finding suitable presents for all of you but I have
been trying my best to make this special so I suggested you might fancy bit of
chocolates but I find it hard to buy individual presents for the family and I hope
that chocolates will be special for you but I think this is really dumb, here's ex-
tra £10 for family spending, the present you can't refuse so please accept it. I
tell you why, you have been a wonderful parents to me also the big brothers to
look after me these years.

I would like to thank to you all for everything you have done for me
and I would like to say that I am very pleased to be here with you all. With-
out any support I wouldn't have been here today. Also I promise you that I
will stay strong and healthy for my big day and that's thanks to you for
great support.

*I just wanted to say that you all have been brilliant lately and I have been
overjoyed about the cuddly hamster, Amie, also thanks for the wicked
Rollerblades.*

You are one in a million I will always love it.

God bless and enjoy, very best wishes, love Thomas XX

We needed no stronger confirmation than that of his positive attitude to
what he was about to undergo. In December, Dan had already written to
him from university that he had a strength and positiveness that he himself
could only dream of. Once again Tom's strong character was making us all
feel very humble.

Chapter 9
Staying Strong

> In the end, strength lies in acceptance, hope is in truth not fantasy; peace cannot be in craving, but in the giving up of desire. (William Horwood, 1987).

Leaving aside the media hype, what exactly *is* a cochlear implant? Cochlear (UK) Ltd describe it for youngsters by likening the cochlea to a piano and imagining the tiny hairs in it playing varying notes, like piano keys that make different sounds, and giving them to the hearing nerve. Playing different groups of notes on a piano is like saying different words to the ear. If everything is working, you can hear but any damage to these little hairs means the cochlea cannot send sound wave messages to the hearing (auditory) nerve. This is when the implant's intricate parts can sometimes help. The outer parts are the microphone which catches sounds and sends them to the speech processor, a small computer which converts sound waves into a special sound code which in turn is sent via the round magnetic transmitter into the inner, unseen parts of the implant. These are the decoder and the electrodes. The former takes the electronic sound wave messages from the microphone and passes them to the electrode rings (which go into the cochlea and act as the substitute for the little hairs) and on to the hearing nerve which transmits the messages to the brain. Then sound is heard.

Unlike a conventional hearing aid, an implant does not amplify sound; it takes it and changes it to a radio signal which is transmitted through the scalp and converted to an electrical current that stimulates the nerves. And, of course, unlike a normal aid, an implant does involve a major operation under a general anaesthetic, and there is always a risk of irreversible damage to the facial nerve. Some limitations in lifestyle also come in its wake, especially partaking in contact sports, and there can be problems with static electricity. It has been said that voices sound electronic or 'robotic' but, of course, hearing people have no way of experiencing that. The device is not switched on until about one month after implantation and that is when the long period of rehabilitation begins.

With this operation it seems the surgery is almost incidental and it is what follows that is so dramatic! Of course, everyone's experience will vary. Pre-lingually deaf youngsters will do very differently depending on the age at which they were implanted. Deafened children or adults implanted quickly after losing their hearing will have very different expectations and outcomes. Before any comparisons are made one needs to know exactly where people are coming from.

After his implant, Tom was dejected and demoralised to read in RNID's *One in Seven* magazine that a young woman was switched on and was 'absolutely overwhelmed at being able to understand speech almost immediately'. I watched his face fall as he read the interview and then I quickly scanned it again myself and realised no mention was made as to how long she had been deaf. However, the name Jenny Burt was familiar and I found another article by her in a newsletter in which she revealed she had been deafened only a matter of months before she had the implant. Very different from Tom's 16 years without sound.

I was concerned enough about what could be a misleading impression, raising some hopes unfairly, to write to the magazine and, as a result, Dawn Egan came to meet us and an article appeared in their 'Relatively speaking' series. We were interviewed separately, Tom with a qualified interpreter present, and Dawn said later it was amazing how much our comments mirrored each other!

At the start of 1996 I was on tenterhooks as we sought to keep Tom fit and well for surgery. It hadn't seemed the ideal time for him to request rollerblades by way of a Christmas present but after the operation we invested in a hefty helmet to go with them! Fed a diet of garlic tablets (a natural antibiotic recommended by our homeopath years ago) and even game enough to suck a whole clove when he hinted at a sore throat in the days immediately prior to D-day, Tom stayed well and 16 January loomed.

Special Support

On the Sunday before, Derek Carpenter, Rector of St George's, who was to become the second incumbent to visit Tom in a hospital, wrote to him:

> As you prepare to go into hospital on Monday I wanted you to know that your very many friends at St George's will be thinking of you and remembering you in their prayers – *I* certainly shall.
>
> We all admire you tremendously for the way in which you manage to overcome what is, I know, a very real disability, and all of us hope and pray that the operation which you have so courageously wanted to take place will be a success. Communication is such an important part of happy living, and I hope that all that will happen in the next few days

will open whole new worlds for you!

But perhaps I can also use this opportunity of saying 'thank you' to you for all that you do for us – and give to us – at St George's. I value what you contribute as part of the serving team, and your regular attendance Sunday by Sunday and your warm smile (which is the best communication of all, and makes us *all* feel better!) make the St George's family better and stronger – so thank you for all that, and for your readiness always to help out and to be involved whenever you're asked. I wish we had another fifty Thomas Froudes!

So good luck and God bless!

Love and best wishes, Father Derek.

Feeling very apprehensive myself I found a prayer that could have been written for us as we set off for the hospital on 16 January.

> Lord, you know the fears and anxieties that fill our hearts at what today will bring. Free us from panic and worry. Anchor our thoughts and minds in your great power and love. Send us into this day with your peace in our hearts and sure confidence in your fatherly care. Through Jesus Christ our Lord, Amen. (Mary Batchelor, 1992).

Tom, meanwhile, had his new pet hamster on his mind. He left us a careful list of instructions on a card headed 'Looking after Amie' to ensure her comfort and safety while he was away from home.

> *To be 100% sure that Amie do not escape while I am away I have placed sticky tape over the exit hole and door. Fresh food and water have been replaced. Enough for over a week. When taking nearer to the cage, be quiet – do not get close too quick or it causes Amie to jump into the tube for safety only if she is sleeping in the tower. Take good care.*

Before leaving for London, the patient-to-be was treated to breakfast in bed at the hospital's designated hour of 7.15 a.m. It was Daniel's favourite old pub glass full of live natural yoghourt/desiccated coconut/honey/vanilla/banana – the Leslie Kenton mix I used to make Tom before he took part in the Super Stars summer sports competition at the local centre. This day held a far more important event – no awards but hopefully a reward one day for all his hard work.

On arrival at GOSH we were caught up in a sea of practicalities. Where to park? How to get a hospital permit. 'What is the number of your car?', asked the issuing office. Of course I hadn't a clue, not being the driver.

And, oh the indignity of it all! Tom, at 6 feet 2 inches, was not built for a bed on Peter Pan ward. We left a member of staff fitting extensions but, due to the serious nature of the operation, Tom was required to spend that night on the main ward rather than the small side room we started in. He swallowed a handful of pre-med pills in one go, much to nurse Netty's amazement. I tactfully suggested removing his huge leather boots so more space became available in our small room but – shock, horror – no! Security, it seemed, was a pair of smelly boots. Left alone to disrobe in private, Tom put the operating gown on *over* his own pyjamas, bless him. Modest to the last! He stayed so calm and self-contained throughout all the preparations.

Outside the hospital it was so noisy. Drills, bangs, clatters, a whole cacophony of building sounds to which he was oblivious. Which, of course, was why we were there . . .

The Waiting Hours

The cochlear implant team psychologist called in to say hallo and some time after noon Father Derek arrived to bless and pray for Thomas who was by then fairly drowsy. He was only just in time as at 1 p.m., earlier than expected, porters came to wheel Tom to the operating theatre. We left him in the anaesthetic room; he was still so calm and brave. I felt such strength coming from him and from his Maker. My prayer was that the surgeon and anaesthetist would make sound judgements. I felt very blessed at that moment and I promised God I would keep that feeling no matter what the outcome of the day. My only request was that Tom would not be brain damaged. I felt I could not pray for the success of the implant at this stage, only for him to come through the surgery safely. (Later I was to regret this reticence to ask for too much . . .) I signed to Tom that he meant the whole world to me and then John and I went to spend some quiet time in the beautiful little hospital chapel.

It was a long, long afternoon. At 5.30 p.m. Netty said everything was going really well and he should be back on the ward in an hour. Kelly, the lovely American audiologist, dropped by and was surprised to learn that we had all slept well the previous night. She had obviously reckoned without the Froudes' fortitude where sleep is concerned! We had told Tom not to hesitate to come in and talk to us if he had any worries and was awake in the night, but he didn't appear. In the morning he said, so politely, 'Sorry I didn't use your service last night!'

At 6.40 p.m. I went down to collect him from the recovery room. The bandage wasn't as huge as I expected but his whole body was shaking uncontrollably, which I found very alarming. It reminded me of the fitting during the meningitis but I was assured it was simply the after-effects of the anaesthetic. He slept all evening.

The surgeon came to see us later and declared it a 'text book' operation. To our surprise and delight they had got all the electrodes in. He was big enough that they had not needed to remove the incus which Kelly had thought he might like to keep as a souvenir since it was 'real neat'. But they *had* cut the nerve of taste, which we were told he 'might or might not notice'. We decided not to mention it.

The following morning I went anxiously to see him at 7 a.m. but he was still fast asleep. Later I learnt that, despite a quiet night, his ear had bled a lot when he moved and this had alarmed him, but he had not been sick. I was sad that no one had alerted me to his distress so that I could have signed and reassured him, since I was sleeping in a side room down the corridor. His neck was stiff and achy when he sat out so he was glad to get back into bed. He found our little inflatable travel pillow helpful to support his heavy, painful head.

An unexpected X-ray was ordered and once he was off the drip he was wheeled down to that department. The bleeding started again, sullying the nice clean floor, and the process seemed painful. He was patient and resigned but I grew more and more concerned about the number of X-rays being taken. I fancied none showed the electrodes in the expected position; they certainly didn't bear any resemblance to the prototype on the wall. When we finally returned to the ward, where they were beginning to think we had got lost, I admitted my fears to a nurse. 'Maybe it'll have to be done again', she hazarded. 'What, the *implant*?' I demanded, horrified. 'No, silly', she smiled, 'the *X-ray*'. I breathed again.

Bad News

Tom's smile returned once or twice but in the main he was very lack-lustre and rather dejected. Luckily he could sleep and I found it ironic to see all the young mums on the ward longing for their restless little ones to nod off while I was aching for Tom to wake up! The following morning I woke early again, needing to see Tom, but he was still sound asleep. By 8 a.m. he was awake and shortly afterwards the surgeon arrived. I had heard her asking urgently for the X-rays and, as she drew the curtains round the bed, I was sure my earlier fears were about to be justified.

The electrodes, it seemed, were not correctly positioned in the cochlea so Thomas would need further surgery. It was referred to as a 'temporary setback' – and I knew it was better that it should be discovered sooner rather than later – but it seemed so unfair when he had been such a perfect patient. And to be discovered just as the sparkle in his eyes and his smile were slowly returning.

We were left alone to digest the bad news. I shed a few tears but Tom was very stoic. I asked him if he was cross or disappointed, 'Disappointed'. I told him he was just too nice to be cross. And the surgeon did admit to a

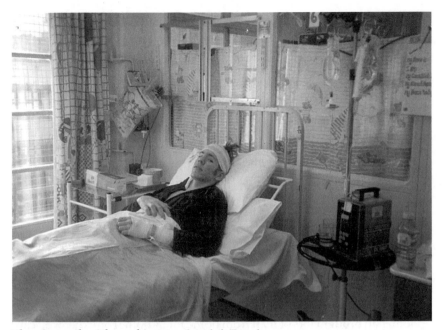

The aftermath of the cochlear implant left Tom low

sleepless night over it, herself. I rang John at work and Jackie at school, both my friend and my boss at that time.

Two of the implant team, Christine and Mary, came to see us and at first didn't believe the news. I only wished I *had* got it wrong. So much for the 'text book op'; maybe it was the page that said how not to do it I thought, somewhat bitterly!

We signed another operation consent form and, thanks to dear Jackie hotfooting it to the hospital after a school faculty meeting, we had a friend to talk to in the late afternoon and news of the outside world. We both finished the day happier than we started it although Tom's temperature was slightly raised.

I slept badly that night and woke at 6 a.m. after a horrible dream in which Tom, a sort of superman in dark school uniform, was standing at an open window, having done something heroic. I went to touch him and although he smiled he was cold to touch and felt distant. He was chubby, as in his first year in senior school. Given the circumstances I knew the dream was easily explained – but nevertheless it left me feeling very shaken.

Four hours later I was feeling really resentful, on Tom's behalf. His ear was paining him and he'd been put on intravenous antibiotics which made him feel very faint. He looked very grey. This was the first time I'd started to wish he hadn't had the implant but I was sure the feeling was only temporary and because he was looking so poorly. It reminded me of that awful black Friday when John came to me and said 'I've just seen Tom'. Just as then, the day was very grey outside.

It was a grim day inside too. Tom went down to theatre at 1 p.m. again. This time we had been led to expect surgery of a far shorter duration but at 3 p.m. were told it would be at least another hour. We found this very unnerving. Approaching 5 p.m. we were distinctly anxious every time the ward phone rang. I was eventually invited to go down with the staff nurse and rescue him from the recovery room. He was only shaking slightly this time. The surgeon apologised again for putting us, and especially Tom, through this second operation but with this one they were really sure the electrodes were correctly sited in the cochlea and not in the large air cells in the mastoid bone as originally.

Because of the added risk of infection Tom had to be put on intravenous antibiotics all weekend and the bandage was to be removed on Monday before an X-ray. Another consultant, who had also been in theatre, came to check Tom's facial nerve was undamaged by getting him to raise a weary smile.

John had brought lots of mail from home for us both. Tom's get well card count was now up to 29 and I had a letter from the Photographer's Gallery with the news that I was a runner-up in the *Observer* 'I wish, I wish' competition. No prizes for guessing what my wish had been! Of course, for Tom to hear my voice after so many years, so what an appropriate day for it to arrive! The first prize was a print of the famous Bert Hardy photograph of his son, Michael, with a real panda which I would have loved, since his other son, Terry, is Daniel's godfather!

At about 8.30 p.m. Tom woke up properly. He said his head felt better than it had before. A croaky throat made his eyes water; he showed a nurse the sign for 'pain'. I asked him if he felt sorry he had the implant. He said 'No', explaining, ' this is horrible but then I can look forward'. I don't think he'll ever know just how much I loved and admired him at that moment.

By Saturday he had spent a good night and despite several blood tests and the intravenous procedures he stayed his usual stoic self. Dan came up on Thameslink from university in Brighton and arrived as Tom was having his antibiotic lines flushed. He brought him a lovely gouache he'd made, with type saying 'Be strong' on it. Tom apologised to his brother for being so down due to the drip. 'I am not myself', he explained sadly.

The pressure bandage, to prevent a haematoma developing, gave tall Tom a distinctly Frankenstein monster appearance as he walked slowly through the ward to the bathroom. Fortunately no tiny people ran

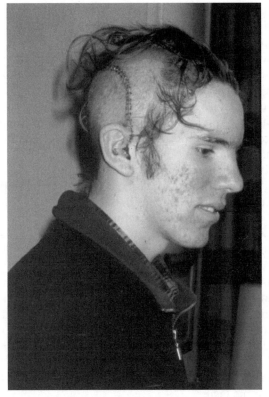

A punk would have been proud of the metal and
the 'Mohican'!

screaming from him! We were told the ten-inch scar would probably be all
the better for being done twice because it was already healing! No drain
was required the second time.

By Sunday Tom's arm was painful from the antibiotics but he perked up
when the drip was removed at 10.15 a.m. just as it was all getting too much
for him. I went to Communion in the hospital chapel. When I returned,
Radio GOSH came to ask him what music requests he had for the day. I
explained . . .

Sometime after his lunch Tom asked me about his tongue and whether it
was that that detected sweet and sour things. I knew then I would have to
tell him about his nerve of taste being severed. I felt awful. He was very
pensive for a while, digesting the information. 'Does it mean I can't taste
my favourite foods?' I could have wept but instead I asked him how he felt

about it. He answered resignedly 'If they were only doing their job, it's all right'. Yet again I was rendered speechless by his maturity.

Our friend on the implant team and two other local teachers of the deaf who have known Tom since he was a baby came to visit us, en route to the Gala Celebration of the twentieth anniversary of the Beethoven Fund for Deaf Children and 'The Life of Ezra Rachlin' at the Savoy Theatre. Later, when they discovered it was to be followed by the television programme 'This is your life' for Ann Rachlin they were tempted to come and 'spring' me from the ward so that I could be there to see it! I doubt I'd have stayed awake though; it had been a *very* long day.

When the bandage was removed on Monday the sight was not as distressing as I'd feared. The scar was held with 27 metal staples and there were just four or five soluble stitches in the ear. The hair being shaved on that side had turned Tom into a semi punk! After the X-ray, which confirmed all was well, and the removal of the wick in his ear, we left the hospital at noon. We had spent seven days there instead of the anticipated two; we were very glad to be going!

Arriving home, armed with Tom's favourite fish and chips for a late lunch, we found a deaf friend on the doorstep. Visibly shaken by Tom's scar he announced what he perceived as an immediate benefit to *us* of the implant, in that Tom would now be able to do the washing up. Our faces must have said it all. 'I'm not allowed to wash up', he explained, 'My wife won't let me; I clatter the plates and cutlery too much!'

Tom was very relieved to be home and wasted no time writing to thank Father Derek for his visit:

> *I wanted to write to you to thank you for the kind letter and visiting me at hospital.*
>
> *You were my very special hospital visitor and I felt really overjoyed to see you and thanks for your blessing before the op. It was real pity that I had 2 operations, so I am recovering well writing you a letter.*
>
> *It was great to see pile of mail waiting for me when I am well enough to get out of bed.*
>
> *I am really looking forward to returning to St. George's because I am really missing my friends badly.*

Various friends from youth club and Junior Church, both youngsters and leaders, came to visit Tom and to hear about his novel experience.

Tom had the rest of the week off school and returned the following Monday, confident enough to cope without the hat we'd bought to save his dignity. On 1 February he had an interview at Croydon College and on 9 February went to GOSH and had the metal staples removed. After three weeks they were well embedded and by the time the last was extricated his face was the colour of the off-white Aran sweater he was wearing. 'Is that the last of the pain?' he asked, weakly.

After that, he couldn't wait for half term to come and what he described as his 'big adventure' – the 'switch on' scheduled for 20 February.

Chapter 10

The Big Adventure

To love is not to give of your riches, but to reveal to others their riches, their gifts, their value and to trust them and their capacity to grow. So it is important to approach people in their brokenness and littleness gently, so gently, not forcing yourself upon them, but accepting them as they are with humility and respect.' (Jean Vanier,1988).

The night before his 'switch on' at Great Ormond Street Hospital, Tom wrote in his diary:

At Youth Club, people asked me if I was nervous about switch on. I said I was-n't and when the time got nearer I got more nervous and really excited. I know I can't expect cochlear implant to be the way I want. It is like I am starting my new life with something new fitted on me. I hope to aim to hear more than aids and able to tell differences. I mean for example I would have liked to hear bell and phone ringing and tell which one I heard.

It seems hard for me to know what sort of sound I could hear until tomorrow because I can't just ask God to make me hear something I want to hear, like hearing people's voice clearly.

We made our way to Great Ormond Street through the chaos caused by a snowfall and the Aldwych bus bomb. (What a coincidence it seemed to learn later that the driver injured in that was himself to be given a cochlear implant to compensate for his shattered hearing.) As we crossed Blackfriars Bridge we saw John Regan, Matthew's godfather, *en route* to King's Reach where he was Deputy Editor of *Woman's Weekly*, on which magazine he and I had worked together for many years. We managed to attract his attention as we stopped and started in the slow-moving traffic and the sight of him seemed like a very good omen. Quite what other commuters made of my shouted explanation – 'He's going to be *switched on!*' – I don't know.

To his father and me, waiting for his first reactions to sound, it seemed an eternity before Tom responded with a puzzled smile (captured by the team on video) and touched the centre of his forehead. He described it as a wave

Tom 'maps' his processor under the guidance of the audiologist at GOSH

travelling across it and echoing in his head. He was disconcerted to find the sounds gave him a headache but Kelly knew exactly how he felt. She remembered being exposed to some incredibly high frequency sounds when she was training and she 'felt' them on her forehead. To Tom, not having heard any *normal* high frequency sounds for so long, they had the same effect, but in a couple of days the sensation passed, although until it did he said he felt all the sounds were 'packed' into his forehead. He asked me 'am I really hearing?' The implant team, used as they were to small children with little or limited language, found all his observations very helpful.

When he heard voices for the first time Tom winced – but then said he could tell the difference between mine and that of the American audiologist, Kelly. And that we were both too loud! Dr Bellman seemed amazed and delighted at such early discrimination, which she said she would not have expected at this stage.

On that first day what are known as the threshold (where one starts to hear) and the comfort (above which it becomes painful) levels were set in record time since Tom was so much older than the average recipient at the children's hospital. Later he did his own 'mapping' on their computer and carefully considered the levels that he was happy with. When some sounds were set too high they gave him earache. It seems to be metallic noises such as those in a kitchen that he hates so it's lucky he didn't plan catering as a career!

When we got home he heard the telephone ringing in the hall and also responded to the grandfather clock, the vacuum cleaner, the loo flushing, the doorbell, the fridge 'humming' and the wind down the chimney. Tom had already started on the detection of sounds. In time we hoped he would learn to discriminate, identify and comprehend them. He admitted to being very nervous initially because he had been afraid he'd have a shock with loud noises. Such was the team's care and concern for him that their cautious mapping was designed to leave him calm and unstressed.

Oddly enough, the Great Ormond Street Hospital series was on television at that time and that evening it was the programme on cochlear implants. It made fascinating viewing, of course, and Tom reacted to the 'beeping' noise in the anaesthetic room. He also seemed fairly envious of the small child who featured in the programme.

The Search for Sounds

That half term was a voyage of discovery for him, exciting but very tiring. We went up to the hospital on three consecutive days, during which he worked with audiologists, a speech therapist and a teacher of the deaf, all involving a lot of structured listening. He was particularly excited by the fact that he could hear 'S' and 'SH' sounds and he listened hard for them along with the other 'lings' – 'aah', 'ee' and 'oo'. Jackie Parsons was invited to the second day's rehabilitation and it was good to have her moral support in that special week. She'd agonised with us over the delays in initial assessment. She'd consoled us when the first implant went wrong and it felt only right she should be part of the early, exciting steps to hearing again.

Each member of the team involved with the rehabilitation wrote an encouraging message in our ring binder, beneath the 'Long time no hear' card which was by then stuck inside the front cover.

By the third day Tom made a point of testing himself at home. He came into the sitting room, closed the door and waited to see if he could hear the grandfather clock chime in the hall. We purposely gave no indication when it started but waited for a few strikes before turning to look at him. He was mouthing the number to himself – 'four, five' – and he was absolutely right! We were all starry-eyed!

Tom sensed other people's expectations were likely to be unrealistic, despite our cautious explanations. On the Saturday evening he said 'I hope they won't expect me to be talking clearly and hearing everything well at church tomorrow'. Once there the following morning he said he could hear but that things sounded different. I pointed out that the vast area with its lofty, arched roof and tiled floor were the reason but he alerted and turned to me enquiringly as soon as the organ started.

I also detected a difference in people's reactions to him. They seemed to be speaking much more carefully and clearly and *expecting* a response. Having watched him grow up deaf their hopes may have exceeded our, more informed, expectations of the implant but, over the course of the next few months, my friends commented on improved communication and better than ever lip-reading on his part. I, in turn, forgot that he was less inclined to 'switch off' from the latter when boredom set in so was surprised when he asked me on one occasion, after I'd finished what I'd fondly imagined was a confidential conversation, what my friend had meant was 'dreadful'.

Back at school for the first time the following day Tom heard the bell ringing. In assembly he was aware of the *silence* in the big hall and knew when the teacher started talking, without looking at her. He admitted to being fed up with what he was hearing in the biology lesson, when chairs scraping on the laboratory floor and a noisy boy irritated him. Hearing the sound of just three pupils turning over pages in the comparative peace of the small unit classroom made him realise what the public exams would be like in the huge wooden hall with hundreds of students doing the same thing and he resolved then and there to switch off!

Jackie, true to her word, took on his rehabilitation in school with the enthusiasm and skill that is her particular trademark and makes her an inspired and inspiring Christian teacher of the deaf. She cleverly got him to listen and discriminate between the names of footballers, characters from the 'East Enders' television soap and between makes of his favourite cars. They also listened to different musical instruments and he was able to talk about the 'resonance' of some.

Although at home we had always tried to remember to include Tom in mealtime and other conversations, after the implant it seemed he himself was far more anxious to be involved and, if we forgot to explain to him, would remind us.

Awareness of Noise

Jane, one of the local speech therapists, who has known Tom since he was in the infants, also worked with him in school after the implant and told me that she so well remembered the way I would always point out sources of sound to him, even though he couldn't hear them. She felt this was really going to stand him in good stead now he had the implant and needed to hear, and eventually differentiate, between a variety of sounds. It

Excited anticipation for what he might feel from the drum kit, Christmas 1986

seemed a far cry to me from the time when he was 18 months or so and, after I had shown him a workman drilling in the road and indicated the type of noise, he would thereafter always react to a striped cone and point hopefully to his own ears, even when work was not in progress! We have a snapshot of him on the pavement at two years old, during a spate of resurfacing work, pretending to be a road roller himself, his little woolly jacket stretched across his two body-worn aids giving him a distinctly pigeon-chested appearance.

We have a friend who became blind as an adult and after Tom had helped in the Maundy Thursday workshop on the huge Holy Week collage she told us she could *see* it if she went up really close to it and if someone *described* it to her. I think this is the same for Tom in many ways; he needs to know what's making the sound and have it described before he can be sure of it. He himself was able to describe the sound of birds in the garden to me one day, when I questioned him, by making a conversational sign which exactly described the 'cheep, cheep' dialogue that was going on, rather than bird *song*, as such. That seemed very perceptive to me.

The biggest breakthrough during the early rehabilitation period was when Tom was on study leave. He was fast asleep on the sofa when I came home from work. I stood about three feet away, made no movement or vibration, but slightly shouted his name and he slowly responded. To see him fighting the intrusive sound and struggling against having to wake up, reluctantly and crossly, was just brilliant! It felt like a huge step forward. I witnessed that, but what I didn't see was his surprise when he opened a new wooden box at home and heard a sound. He shut the lid and the sound stopped. He repeated the actions and slowly realised it must be a musical box. The sound was quite soft and was totally unexpected for him, which was why he reported it, in amazement, on my return.

It wasn't until June the following year that Tom made a new friend who had a cochlear implant at the same age as him. He went on an FYD First Aid weekend at Rotherhithe Youth Hostel in Docklands and he and Lisa compared notes and had what he called 'a great talk about the operation'. She seemed to be able to hear about the same things as him and it was really good for him to have a friend with the same experiences. We later discovered that Jackie had been her teacher when she was in infant school. The Deaf world is a small world!

Eighteen months after switch-on Tom completed his implant diary and made some comments on the aesthetics of the device. He found the leads from microphone to processor annoying and wrote 'I wonder if they could develop a microchip size without processor to wear on our body? Sounds too futuristic . . . ?' Maybe it did at the time but he went on to design a poster for Cochlear UK of what he'd like to see as the implant of the future (and won the prize in his age group). In 2001 his dream came true and he was allowed an ESPrit 22 mini-processor which fits above the ear and, unbelievably enough, contains not one but *two* maps! Gone are the processor in its pouch at his waist and the long leads that so bugged him and cramped his sense of style. The ESPrit is beautifully unobtrusive but gives him the sounds he needs.

Background Material

It was fascinating for us to attend Professor Graeme Clark's lecture at the Royal College of Surgeons in January 2001. The quietly charismatic Australian professor, a very Christian man who confessed he went away to weep alone in a disused laboratory after his first patient heard with the multichannel cochlear implant, told us some of the history of his invention. Alluding to the bulk of the first speech processor, which in his projected slides resembled a built-in oven in shape and size, he explained how his technicians had assured him that they could reduce its dimensions – to something the size of a sewing machine which the implantee could drag around with him! That brought home to me the advances which now benefit Tom since 20 years on he was in front of me (so he could see the interpreters) sporting a new mini-processor which was almost invisible from where I was sitting. And hearing with it!

On that memorable occasion it was especially good to see the unstinting time and support that the inimitable Tricia Kemp of the Cochlear Implanted Children's Support Group (CICS) has given countless parents, including us, over many years, acknowledged when she received the Gold Cochlear Badge from Professor Clark. The implant, she declared in her acceptance speech, is 'as close to a modern day miracle as we are likely to go'.

Professor Clark's book *Sounds from Silence: The Bionic Ear Story* (2000) describes its birth and development and makes fascinating reading, most of it within the reach of a lay person. I particularly warmed to him when I read that he became

> even more aware of how useful Sign Language of the Deaf has been, and that some children, for various reasons, will still need to acquire this skill. For example, having the implant at an early age doesn't preclude children from learning to sign in order to supplement their new-found auditory skills and to communicate with signing family and friends.

I myself feel sad that the Deaf community should still appear to feel so threatened by cochlear implants.

Tom, I know, wishes he had been able to have one when he was small. Selfishly, because he was so easygoing and so rewarding, I can't help wondering how different his personality might have been with what I think must be the added pressures it involves. All that listening and speaking, the speech therapy, the hospital visits and procedures, the initial mapping which may span several months for a tiny child, the concentration and ongoing rehabilitation, to say nothing of all the problems with static electricity and safety in what should be normal, carefree, childish pursuits. Depending on the policy at hospital and at school, signing may or may not be taboo with an implant. I feel with his signing Tom's own good language could not have been bettered in primary school, even with an early implant, although I realise the quality of his speech would have improved. More importantly, I am not sure that, following the trauma of the meningitis and the assault his young brain suffered, we would have been able to hand Tom over to a surgeon at a tender age for invasive surgery without a life-threatening reason for doing so.

Happily for me I did not have to make the decision. I am, in a way, 'let off the hook', because the adolescent Thomas made it for himself. The Deaf community cannot criticise me – and should not criticise him. As a family we love, respect and enjoy Tom exactly the way he is and would have him no different. We realise that he has received the implant too late for it to be very useful in making his own speech clearer or for him to understand what people are saying to him simply by listening. His lip-reading has always been brilliant but he admits that when he is concentrating on it he feels he is not really 'listening' as well. However, environmental sounds are important to us all and the implant has put him in touch with the world around him, exactly as we had hoped. Simply to see him turn to an unexpected cough or sneeze behind him is still a delight! Equally, though, because of the duration of his deafness and the strategies he developed for dealing with a silent world, he is not fazed when, for any reason, he has to be without the processor. That, in some ways is a comfort, but the fact that he uses it all his waking hours, even six years after implantation, means that, despite its limitations, it holds much meaning for him. In fact, he tells me that sometimes even when it is off at night in bed he feels he is still *hearing* – what he refers to as a 'flash-back' feeling. This makes me wonder if it is rather like a lost limb still causing pain/feeling to an amputee.

When the Deaf community campaigns against cochlear implants and warns that implanted children may grow up and question the right of their parents to take such decisions for them I concede that is their valid, albeit limited, point of view. But I think they should also ask themselves about those children denied the chance of an implant by their carers who might, just might, grow up and ask *why* didn't you allow me one? For them, by then, it will be too late. An implant does not turn a deaf person into a hearing person. With the processor off there is no sound; any residual hearing in that ear will have been destroyed by the operation. A return to silence and signing is possible at any time and surely the Deaf community should be big enough to support and embrace the individual in any circumstances. I cannot help but agree with deaf American writer Tom Bertling's warning in his book *A Child Sacrificed to the Deaf Culture* (1994) that 'parents should cast a cautious eye towards anyone wanting to *sacrifice a deaf child towards preserving a culture'*.

Range of Experience

Deaf people like Tom have a valid viewpoint to put across and can do so from an informed position. Tricia Kemp, other friends and the hospital all offer his name as a contact for appropriate prospective implantees of his age so that he can tell it like it is, or like it has been, for him. He has also written of his feelings in 'Cochlear implants: a collection of experiences of users of all ages' (National Cochlear Implant Users' Association, 2001).

Fortunately, not all deaf people disapprove. Our friend Rosemary wrote to me after his operation that it was 'wonderful to hear Thomas' success on cochlear transplant (sic). He is the most luckiest boy, to have a wonderful, understanding, encouraging mother. I admire your attitudes.'

That letter was as gratifying for me to read as it was to hear a young deaf worker, from an educational establishment where the majority of pre-schoolers appear to be implanted, say that when two children of similar age were implanted at the same time, it was the child with signing skills who 'took off' afterwards and would 'talk, talk, talk' while the child without the benefit of that manual language lagged far behind. Food for thought there, then!

Because of my personal feelings about Tom as a toddler and despite hearing him tell the parents of a deaf 17-month-old (a carbon copy of him at the same stage) that he wished he'd had an implant at that age 'because then I wouldn't be the way I am now', I continued to have great reservations about early implantation. But having seen how well that same little boy (implanted seven months after meeting Tom) does with his, thanks I am sure to the early signing he shared with his hearing parents and two sisters both before and after it, I am slowly coming round to the idea.

On what was to be our very last visit to Great Ormond Street Hospital we shared the waiting room with the parents and teachers of an enchanting two-year-old in a snowsuit who was being 'switched on' that week. My eyes filled with tears as I envisaged the future ahead of him, of his being able to hear and develop his own speech. Across the busy, crowded little room Tom noticed my damp eyes and asked me what was wrong. And at that moment I realised nothing was wrong. Our experience was different – but if it had resulted in a teenager who could spot another's subtle distress and care enough to query it then everything was very definitely all right.

Tom's audiological scientist at the UCL has recognised pre-lingually deaf implantees of his age need a different sort of ongoing support and, with her colleagues, is hoping to be able to address this in a constructive and mutually beneficial way. She sees them as a small and special group and feels 'we will not see their like again'. With children being implanted at a younger age those teenagers who require an implant will likely be ones who have been recently deafened, whose speech and language has, of course, been perfectly normal. They will have different traumas to cope with if illness or accident has destroyed their hearing but they will not have been coping with pre-lingual deafness all their lives.

By the time Tom had outgrown Great Ormond Street and transferred to the UCL Adult Programme at the RNTNE Hospital in Gray's Inn Road,

London, we had, in a way, come full circle as the building also houses the Nuffield Centre where he was first seen and given hearing aids at the age of one year. It sometimes feels that a lifetime of experience has been packed into those 21 years.

Chapter 11

Language for Life

It was the language born of hands that was my beginning. (Ruth Sidransky, 1990).

Exactly as Penelope Lively wrote, in lovely, thought-provoking words which seemed so tailor-made to front this book, 'language tethers us to the world'. And no matter what form that language takes, from voice or hand, from lips or eyes, from this ethnicity or that culture, it is our lifeline. Most of us will have experienced the inadequacy we feel in a foreign country the language of which is alien to us. Even with a smattering of knowledge, we feel lost in a sea of uncertainty, inadequate, frustrated, impotent, possibly even panicky.

That is exactly how a deaf child could so easily feel, countless times a day. And that is why he or she needs access to words (preferably, in my view, via signs) so that language gets going as quickly as possible. By his own development over 20 years, Tom has proved to me that, along with access to our family food, foibles and folklore, he also had access to our family language, via our lip patterns and the English signs we learnt and used. He had, in those early months of toddlerhood, nearly the same chance as a hearing child to discover that things had names. By the time he was 30 months he knew and used over 80 signs regularly:

yes, no, biscuit, bread, porridge, ice cream, drink, wait, very, good, bad, milk, naughty, ball, dirty, clean, up, down, upstairs, Mummy, Daddy, Grannie, more, where, jumping, chair, car, fire, train, shops, under, over, fork, spoon, spider, open, baby, cat, dog, elephant, giraffe, sheep, pig, horse, mouse, rabbit, fish, same, bring, duck, bird, water, hot, cold, book, helicopter, aeroplane, fall, stop, go, thank you, please, hello, careful, walking, telephone, tree, big, small, bye-bye, school, moon, sun, writing, painting, home, sorry, chair, light, coat, hat, come, banana and orange.

I suspect that was very much on a par with a hearing child's vocabulary at a similar age, whereas with deaf children Marschark (1993) reports that even the best pupils on the best oral programmes are rarely beyond ten words at the age of two-and-a-half years. And for Tom that was just the start. In no time at all he was soaking up new language like a sponge. He was able to hold a pen perfectly at a very young age and demonstrated excellent control of it. Once at school, before he learnt to read and write, he would cover pages in 'scribble talk', beautifully formed cursive script that conveyed absolutely nothing! This concerned the unit head and she asked a clinical psychologist to see him. He saw no cause for alarm and I personally think it was simply that Tom was rehearsing what he'd do once his real reading and writing skills developed. He obviously took great pleasure in doing it and the fact that it was meaningless to us didn't make it any less important to him. It certainly didn't suggest any worrying, underlying cause to me and, in fact, at one stage his reading age level was actually above his chronological age, something which everyone was at pains to point out couldn't be sustained for long. I have a delightful sketch he did for his daddy of a matchstick type man with the caption 'vae vae goo boy!' That seemed to affirm his ability to lip-read and even suggest an idea of phonics, within limits.

In *Language for Ben* (1987) Lorraine Fletcher wrote about her son, 'Having been born deaf, Ben's natural perception of the world is that of a deaf person. He thinks in pictures, using highly developed visual skills.' She also felt his attention span only developed when he worked with a deaf BSL user in the nursery. Tom's attention only ever had to be sought if he was totally engrossed in play. Otherwise he was always watching like a hawk! Later, he even seemed to have the almost unnerving ability to watch me out of the corner of his eye if I was fingerspelling a word for him, and copy it down correctly, to my absolute amazement.

Born Hearing

Having been born hearing, of course, Tom's early days were different from Ben's. It's hard, and sometimes painful, for me to remember those early, pre-meningitic days. Snapshots show a happy little family, delighting in its new addition, basking in the sun of a summer filled with sweetness. A third son, and one I was planning to have time to enjoy to the full. Nervous with Matthew, because after all one only *practises* on the first baby, coming closer to coping with Daniel but weak after the complications following his birth and busy with his older brother who was not yet walking when he was born, by the time Tom arrived both his siblings were at school and I had daytime hours in which to relish this easygoing infant. Like the baby in the beautiful passage from Eva Figes' book *The Knot* (1997) Thomas was wrapped in a cloud of language.

I talk to him constantly, my sweet William. It seems as natural as breathing. The words are a kind of lullaby, as I walk him up and down, as I see his eyelids rising and falling, rising and falling, soothing him. I lull him on a cloud of soft language, it wraps him round, comforting him. Through it he knows I am nearby, holding him, shielding him from the terror of unending chaos, a limitless vacuum of random sounds into which he was thrust so suddenly.

Each time his eyes open, I speak to him. I know he is listening intently. I know it by the slight frown puckering his brows, by the manner in which he tries to focus his new eyes to where the sound is coming from. His new blue eyes which have not yet found their colour, reflecting sky, not earth. My mouth has found its song, and I sing it unthinkingly, for him. I am not conscious of sounding foolish, even if, overheard, the words seem silly. It is for him I speak, in the language of the newly born. He must hear it now, his mother tongue.'

That is why I have a 'gut' feeling that Tom's 'English' language (despite the odd hiccups here and there, mainly now in tenses and in omitting function words like 'the' and 'a') is due to the fact that he was hearing the mother tongue *in utero* for 12 to 20 weeks, if current foetal research is right, and certainly for 20 weeks *after* birth. If a four-day-old baby can distinguish the speech of its native language it would seem to me that language can be absorbed before and after birth. Indeed, as Truman W. Stelle points out in *A Primer for Parents with Deaf Children* (1982) 'by the time the (hearing) child is about six months old and begins to babble, he has been exposed to, and has been quietly storing away, a tremendous amount of spoken language'. Even deaf babies babble at first and a 'naming explosion' starts with hearing children at about 18 months when some toddlers start to put words into sentences. From then on it seems that six to ten new words are added to the child's vocabulary each day.

The case for prior linguistic knowledge is well made in a fascinating chapter in *Baby It's You* by Annette Karmiloff-Smith (1994). Noam Chomsky is frequently quoted on his belief that each child has an innate language and that children are in a way 'programmed' for language as 'pre-set and pre-wired as a tape recorder', able to recognise the complex rules of syntax and grammar and with a special organ for the comprehension of language. On 3 January 1999 the *Observer* reported on research contributing to the continuing argument among linguists over whether children do learn in this way. The *Science* paper from Gary Marcus and colleagues at the Department of Psychology at New York University came close to endorsing Chomsky's view from the 1950s, 'They gradually learn to fit their parents' language into this linguistic hardware package'. And Marc Marschark who, over the past 20 years, has made a study of deaf children's language and cognitive development and whose brilliant books I have only recently discovered, has found that 'prenatal auditory experience can exert powerful effects on postnatal learning and perception'. (Marschark, 1993).

As nothing more than a lay person with a vested interest, I would like to see research done on language acquisition by born deaf children and those pre-lingually deafened after birth. I feel it could well suggest that BSL is the genuinely natural, first language of the former group but that Signed English could be more akin to the first language of the second group. But I know I lay myself open to a huge amount of criticism by merely making such a suggestion, which will be seen as heresy in many quarters. The politics of deafness are such that hearing parents of deaf youngsters are not only caught up in the Oralism v Signing debate but also in the BSL v SE/SSE one. Having read all the arguments for and against all methods, and from our personal experience, I still truly feel that a pre-lingually deafened baby does not simply relinquish an aptitude for English but that, with total communication it can be fostered, and I feel that English was, and remains, Tom's first language. In the many hours I have watched him asleep, for example, I have never once seen him sign in his dreams!

Bilingualism aims to give deaf children English as a second language, after BSL, and if one has to go down this route I think it is very important for growing up in a hearing world. I know Deaf users of BSL have a wonderful, living language literally at their fingertips but when it is to the exclusion of any English it can only result in a low level of English literacy. That rules out much in the way of meaningful communication via Minicom text phone conversations between two deaf people or RNID Typetalk BT Telephone Relay Service ones between deaf and hearing people. It also inhibits the satisfactory reading of subtitles, newspapers, letters, books, vital instructions on electrical goods, machinery or medicines, notices, recipes, invitations, danger and road signs, the highway code, maps, holiday brochures, catalogues, reports and emails. It makes filling in application and booking forms a difficult, confusing and worrying task and necessitates enlisting outside help, at the expense of true independence.

Whatever the prevailing politics, it is an inescapable fact that 'reading and writing form an essential link to the worlds of social and cognitive interaction, and the consequences of illiteracy have increasing impact on all realms of functioning as deaf children grow up' (Marschark, 1993).

Desire to Communicate

Tom's own desire to communicate stems, I feel sure, from his early exposure to signing. If, as Marschark (1993) suggests, 'early training with a manual form of English could be particularly beneficial for the reading abilities of such children, giving them the advantages of early exposure to language and English-relevant experience', I think it would follow that it led to him wanting to express himself on paper.

Pam Gallagher, a teacher at the Royal School for Deaf Children, Margate, tells me that she cannot imagine teaching English without Signed English. 'It is a most invaluable tool without which it would be impossible to put over the finer points of grammar, structure, etc.' She herself is one of the best exponents I've met; her SE embodies all the best of BSL in its fluidity and expression. Because it has a low profile in the annals of sign, there are no books extolling its virtues and some people are happy to dismiss SE as 'visual nonsense'. However, Wendy Mears reminds users that

> The visual message presented through the signed aspect of SE must be consistent with the rules of BSL in terms of placement, direction, non-manual features etc. and must have clear identity with the meaning of the English which it accompanies.

What's more, those taking Signed English exams must have first gained a pass in at least CACDP Stage One BSL and to my mind that puts its allegiance to, and acknowledgement of, that language clearly in perspective. Signed English manuals and dictionaries and CD Roms may be obtained from the Working Party for Signed English, and the Marathon dictionaries are available from the London Borough of Bromley.

Jane Douglas, a deaf friend who is a qualified psychodynamic therapist and counsellor, brought up orally following meningitis as a toddler, but now a sign language user, stresses that parents' early reactions to deafness and their acceptance of the condition play a crucial role in the development of their child. A positive reaction will stand the child in good stead; a negative one, based on denial, could all too easily lead to psychological, mental and emotional problems later. A flexible approach to communication is, she maintains, beneficial to everyone concerned and it should be the child's needs rather than what the professionals, or even the parents, want, that should be the important, deciding factor.

If early communication within the family is crucial to the child's development, so is the need for interaction elsewhere as the youngster grows up and Tom's obvious desire to 'speak' to the outside world via letters or emails seems a natural progression.

Making Contact

Growing up with Signed English and Sign Supported English meant that Tom could write letters, which kept him in touch with people he couldn't phone or chat to, face to face, and late-night notes to the family which never ceased to delight us. With his permission I make no apology for sharing some, warts and all, here. Marschark (1993) reports Wilbur (1977) as arguing that 'word omission, as well as many of the other errors evident in deaf children's writing, results from their failure to adopt a 'discourse orientation'. She suggested that for them writing was often seen as a 'laborious, sentence-by-sentence task, rather than an attempt at verbal communication'. I can't help feeling that in Tom's case his writing belies the truth of this observation, as it does to the 'general conclusion that the average deaf 18-year-old writes on a level comparable to that of a hearing 8-year-old' (Kretschmer & Kretschmer, 1978) as quoted by Marschark (1993).

By the age of ten, Tom was writing to his godmother, not a prissy, two-line, bread-and-butter thank-you letter after Christmas but a really chatty one, full of his news. And all without any prompting or pressure.

Dear Anne and family,
Thank you very much for Naturetrail Omnibus Book. How kind of you. I love it so much. Sometime I read it lots of time. Do you have a lovely time? I had lovely Christmas. I was torch at Christmas. When I come home I run to present quickly because it will be excited. I hope Emily had lovely time. Emily is very smartly (dressed) for nursery school. I love Emily's coat for school. Soon I have to left my school because I am grow-up. I will go to new school soon. I will sent you a photograph of me with my new school. Very soon I will go on little holiday with my school for 1 week. I am going to Isle of Wight with my school. I am looking forward I think I will have lovely time. When I left my friend will write they names on my school shirt to help me to remember my friend. When it is my last day at school I will have a big fun party at school for me because I am lefting soon. When I go to my new school I will have lots of home and school work to do at home and school. I hope Emily enjoy her time and have a nice time. Thank you very much for the letter it was lots of writing on a card. I hope you have a great fun and good time. I will give you big huyg and BIG HUG lots of kiss.
Lots of love from Thomas xxxx

Very far from perfect, admittedly, but a lively piece of communication, I felt.

Despite Marschark (1993) quoting Webster (1986) suggesting that 'one reason why deaf children fail to make use of discourse structure in their writing is that they lack the rules of conversation normally acquired from monitoring ongoing verbal interactions' I could see the 14-year-old Tom

Wearing the 'lefting' shirt after his last day at
Primary school

also had a lovely way with words when writing to his sorely-missed
brother at university. His teasing humour came over in the first lines!

*Dear Whatever the name is?? Oh dear I seem to have lost your name. I am not
used to your name very much lately. Erm, let say you are Danny. Righto.*

Dear old Dan,
*I am missing you so much. How ya doing?? One night Mum, Dad, Matt had
huge pizza for dinner. Ha, Ha you missed it. I planned to send you leftover piz-
zas in with your letter. Changed my mind. I have sent you a tiny crumb of pizza.
Oh dear seem to have lost it, it only weighted nothing, Not worth it eh.*

*Today I am unwell, have been off school for 3 days, 1 day is Baker Day and 2 is
absent. Righto, 2 of my teacher is off work so mum had to leave me at home alone
so I did well – this is my 2nd time. I am not scared eh.*

*When are you gonna to come home to your little bruv?? It is my turn to call
you something. Erm . . . The Cool Chappie. Burp!! Sorry, seem to be having too
much to eat today.*

After such a close relationship down the years small wonder Tom missed his brother when he went away to university

> *Guess what, one weekend you know what time Grand Prix live is on at night? No? Yes? No? Yes? No? Sorry – 3.15 am. I got up at 3.15 watched it finished at 5.30 YAWN zzzzZZZ . . . Arghh . . . sorry I was asleep.*
>
> *What else is there to tell about. Erm . . . ? Do you watch EastEnders some nights, No? Yes? No? Yes. It is all about Grant & Phil all night. No else bit of Sharon and Cindy. Most of them is always Grant and Phil.*

(Two sketches, one of a punk and one with what Tom captioned 'hair overgrown' adorned the side of the page as he tried to speculate on what style Dan would be sporting on his next trip home).

A deliciously chatty style came across when writing to the brother he missed so much, but it was compassion that was to the fore when he wrote to the ailing Roy Castle. Although Tom was a huge fan of the 'Record Breakers' television programme and we told him when cancer was diagnosed in its presenter, it was not until he saw Roy, bald from the chemotherapy, on the News that it really sunk in. Maybe, like another Thomas before him, he had to *see* to believe. After watching the interview which so shocked and distressed him he couldn't settle until he'd written:

Dear Roy,
Hello, my name is Thomas Froude. I am profoundly deaf. I used to watch you on

the programme. I really like you. I felt so sorry for you. I used to watch you on programme every Friday after school. I liked to watch great facts. You look really different. But I don't want to tell about your hair because I might hurt your feelings. I am really sorry about you. I hope you don't die. I have been praying every night by my bed.

    Good luck but don't die, for me. You are so great person.

    Lots of love from Thomas.

In return he received a treasured letter and photograph from Roy Castle and we were all devastated when, during a holiday in Northumbria, we heard the news of his death, on the car radio.

When Dan came home from Brighton for Christmas he was treated to a set of clues compiled by his young brother, with which to locate his present:

To Dan

You have 2 secs to find your own present now. Only kidding Ha Ha.

RULES 1) Do not open the sealed paper on the back of each clue, leave it for afterward

2) When you do have all clues you found come downstairs and do the message on floor.

3) Say 'Rules are Rules; Info by Santa Claus.

> Clue 1 *You will be able to find next clue in the stocking with 'Noel' on it.*
>
> Clue 2 *Do you read me? You will find the next clue in a wine bottle above window in your room.*
>
> Clue 3 *I think I can hear you puffing. Come down.*
>
> Clue 4 *You are doing well. Your last clue is: Where do I keep going and play with trains. You need to look up when you see Clue 5.*
>
> Clue 5 *Go downstairs and look in video cupboard. You must have less than 12 guesses which box it is in or your game is over. I am only kidding it is not last clue, I will keep you busy.*
>
> Clue 6 *I think you have got all 5 clues already. Right turn all the clues facing down and peel the paper off and there are 2 letters missing. You must add it and go where it says it would be under something . . . Don't forget to put it in order and MERRY CHRISTMAS.*

Told by his teacher when Tom was a toddler that we all need language for sequencing (putting our thoughts and plans in a logical order) I could see how Tom's signs had led not only to his brain working but to a delight in language and its use. It would have been easy for a young teenager to simply wrap a parcel and secrete it under the Christmas tree, like the rest of us, but he chose to turn it into a word game. Sadly, I can no longer remember what it was Dan discovered at the end of all this inventive discourse. I can, however, remember what Tom had for Christmas in 1994. He had already negotiated his present by way of a long missive to us:

> *To Mum and Dad,*
> *I don't really know how to say this, I suppose this is bit early to tell you this. I think I know what you are going to say, but I really would like to get myself new bike. Don't be surprised, I have reasons why, here is some:*
>
> * *I am losing bit of interests on my bike now*
> * *I want to have new start (do you understand?) It is little bit like having new fresh start at school, start again properly (some thing I want)*
> * *I realise that my bike seems to be smaller than Dan's*
>
> *If I was to buy new bike I will buy cheaper one (mountain bike) less attractive (I mean not easy for boys to see then start to steal it). I will save up some and buy it myself. I think it can be for Xmas? If you prefer to buy it bit later, I don't mind if you say No I can understand. I hope you understand, Thanks, you are the only person to talk to, love Thomas, sleep tight.*
> *P.S. If I will buy bike I will stop buying video games. I know I am lucky. Please don't think that I am selfish. I will stop. Promise.*

In 1995 Tom, completely off his own bat, wrote a page for the parish magazine. I felt it carried a subliminal message about loneliness and it made me sad but it prompted a lovely letter from a friend in the congregation.

THOMAS FROUDE WRITES
I would like to say to all how great St. George's is.

I suppose you know that I am profoundly deaf and I have been a member of St. George's for all of my life. My mum brought me on Palm Sunday when I was just two weeks old and I was baptised here 3 months later.

I think Fr Derek and Fr Robert are Brilliant. Fr Robert is a great person to joke with because I think he can be witty. They both have great sense of humour and are very understanding because they know how to communicate with me, they are my great friends that I will never forget.

I am really pleased to be here with all of you. St. George's is part of my life that I could look back when I was young, all of memories I have. I still do activities at St. George's. I used to go to Cubs, Adventurers, Junior Youth Club and now I am a member of the new Senior Youth Club and I am really enjoying it very much, same as Junior Youth Club with Bob and Chris of course. I still go to Scouts and I am the Patrol Leader of 6th Beckenham South but soon I will be leaving Scouts because I am nearly 15 and a half years old. I am a server. I began when I was young starting as boat boy then torch, Acolyte and I am now Crucifer. Joan Conway trained me to do those jobs and I understood most of them. I like serving at Church because I enjoy it. I am a helper at Junior Church and every year I help at the Maundy Thursday Workshop.

I am really enjoying my life with St. George's. I have made a lot of great friends such as Louise, Jonathan, Gerard but I have other grown-up friends of course. I really enjoy myself with friends from St. George's Scouts and Senior Youth Club better than being with my deaf friends because I get a lot of experience being with hearing friends.

Everyday I kept thinking 'I prefer to be with my friends from St. George's.' Sometimes I hope to bump into someone I know from St. George's in Bromley after school. It did happen a few times but not often.

What would my life be like without St. George's? I think I would really like to say thank you to my friends for being here with me at St. George's, that is what friends are for. What more can I say? Friends at St. George's are my special friends. I hope this makes sense to all of you. I feel like presenting St. George's with a Gold Award for best Church I ever visited!

I love you all, from Thomas Froude (aged 15).

Dear Thomas.

I have read and re-read your beautiful letter to us all at St. George's and want to thank you personally for it.

I have known you all your '15 years' and feel proud of you and have watched you grow up and fulfil all the numerous duties you have done in the Church. Thank you for this . . . we need to have young people like you with us all the time. You have a very special family and *we* also love *you* very much – please remember that! With love, Sylvia W.

As the teenagers at the church youth club grew older communication was less easy and Tom would often come home rather downcast. When a friend popped in to the club and happened to observe later that the sight of the teenagers all sitting around and chatting had put him in mind of a gentleman's club I figured I knew why. Once the sporty, physical activities were replaced by earnest conversations impossible for him to follow fully Tom obviously couldn't help feeling left out.

Others may not always have taken Tom's feelings into account but he himself was frequently sensitive in certain situations. Wendy, who's been the best of friends to us ever since Dan was a toddler, lost both her mother-in-law and her husband, Brian, in a short space of time. Tom wrote to her about the former 'I am very sorry about your husband's mother. I shall felt sorry for your husband. What bad news for you. Oh dear. I felt upset about it.'

When Brian was dying of mesothelioma, just before Tom's fifteenth birthday, Tom wrote a note imploring me to tell Wendy

> that there is no need to send me a present because I know the state Wendy had been through and there is no need to send me anything. I understand how Wendy is coping, tell her not to worry about my birthday. Save a penny. Tell her no present or anything thank you. No need to be sorry or ashamed.

The following Christmas, just prior to his implant, Tom finished his long thank you letter to her with 'I hope you enjoyed Christmas and I know it must have been hard to enjoy Christmas without Brian. I hope it is ok for me to say that'.

That summer we had visited our friends Barbara and Terry Hardy in their old converted farmhouse high in the Auvergne. Tom loved the holiday at Maison Seule and wrote on our return:

> I would like to write you a thank you letter. I wanted to tell you how much I have enjoyed my holiday spending time with you and the 2 dogs of course. I was really impressed with your work on your new house and hope it goes well. Working and being your slave had put me off going home because I liked working there. Also I am missing my French atmosphere and food as well. Now I am missing Charlie and Holly and I was hoping to see them in next morning.
>
> I think I will end the letter here. Keep up all good work and the very best luck and hope it goes well. Hope to visit you again when it is completed. Hope Charlie and Holly have learnt the truth that we have gone. Best wishes, love from Thomas.

Barbara replied 'it is great to see a letter from Thomas, it is just as if he is talking to us, and as we can't understand his sign language it is great to 'hear' him talking through a letter.' In the same way his emails were also a revelation to his friend Edna, the stage manager alongside whom he painted at the Players. They showed him in a different light and via them she was able to appreciate his hitherto unsuspected sense of humour. Delighted at the new form of communication she decided to return the sign language book I'd loaned her, although I couldn't resist pointing out that, were a piece of scenery about to fall on his head, a sign would be speedier than an email to alert him to the fact!

Tom frequently left notes on our bed and many's the midnight chuckle we've had at his latest missive. They ranged from simple 'room service' requests – 'will you please kindly make me a coffee in the morning' to a plaintive plea for understanding:

Mum, I don't know how to say this – I think you wouldn't like this. I feel like I want to resign from server's rota and I feel I have some reasons for this.

As you may have noticed my moods every Sunday for some time – this is because sometimes I get bit moody about what I have not done which I wished I should have did it – this is my lack of confidence. My main reason is I am starting not to enjoy as I can't follow very well.

Church is not my thing at the moment but I can go to Church at special service like Xmas etc. I hate being a 'quiet boy' at the end of service.

If you will accept this I want to hand in my resignation after tomorrow service. We can talk about this tomorrow if you want to. Sorry to upset you. Am I old enough to do what I want?

Love you always, love Tom xx

A teenager's natural reluctance to be singled out as 'different' meant that by this time Tom was no longer comfortable to have me sign for him in church and I had, reluctantly, to respect his feelings even though his initial refusal to look in my direction was hurtful. Which is why it is a delight to me, now that he is in his twenties, that he has enjoyed an Alpha Course with deaf people and an interpreter and is keen to pursue this within a local group.

On a different note altogether, years earlier, he had obviously taken exception to something Dan had done and showed that he was certainly not in awe of his big brother. 'Do that again and I'll bring you down like a bloodhound' he threatened on one of his famous notes! But now, with Dan away from home, he kept him abreast of his doings:

Dear Dandy, Hi Dandy.

How ya doing Maty. How would you like your letter from me? In different language? In different language? OK, I will use the outer space lang. Whooah Drewhy it means Hello Dan. Nah. Back to normal now. Erm . . . Ah what was on 14th Feb?? Can't remember, was it your birthday, Dan? Ohhh, Valentine Day, did you get one, I got thousands. Ha.

On Thursday something really horrid happened in the morning when I was on my way to school. As I was getting off the 61 bus at the bus stop, a boy called Alan got off and there was no cars coming opposite of where the bus was going. The car behind the bus overtake the bus because there was no cars so the boy didn't check for incoming cars on both ways, he ran a car knocked him down, I was a witness of whole scene. I ran to help him, his shoes flew in the air in different places, he got blood on his face it was horrible. Luckily a teacher was on the bus and helped him. He was lucky to be alive, because when he was run over he landed on the pavement. I ran to school office to report of whole scene before I went to school office a nurse was driving and she pulled over to help. It was shocking for me seeing it happening. I can't bear to think how bad it could be.

He was taken to hospital. The teacher who helped him was really pleased with me.

(Tom's letter was accompanied by a very detailed series of explanatory sketches; I think he would make an excellent witness!)

The fact that 'deaf children generally are not expected to exhibit much diversity or creativity in the linguistic realm' as, unless they have deaf parents, they are rarely exposed to such characteristics outside school (Marschark, 1993) is not borne out by my observation of Tom's writing.

He was determined to keep in touch with his old friend Caroline, across the world in Australia, although when she came back to England for the first time he was very uncommunicative and shy with her. That was sad to see since they had been such good pals but I think it was just the age he was. Now she is back and living locally they are firm friends again and enjoy socialising. She, just as she did when he was in junior school, has introduced him to a new group of her hearing friends.

In June 1997 he wrote to her in Adelaide:

I think it should be me that should be apologising because I haven't written for so long. I hope you have enjoyed your stay in England, and sorry if I was not the boy you expected me to be like since you left as I can see that I have changed so much. I feel I am not so confident kid as I used to be. I was so nervous when my mum left me to deal for myself to welcome you by myself which I never have experienced before.

I am really working hard to get my confidence back because you might have noticed that I am shy. I have been involved with FYD (Friends for young deaf people) courses – like last April I went away on 3 day Initiative Training at Dorking course to learn about Team working and to build my self-confidence doing Tasks like problem solving (this does not involve sports). This summer in July I am going on Post-Initiative Training at Bude in Cornwall (same place where I stayed for activity Holiday but this time it will be different).

Recently on 6th June I went on 2 day First Aid Training weekend which was brilliant. I stayed at Rotherhithe Youth Hostel by the River Thames. At the end of the Training course I was absolutely worn out by my screaming fans, would you like to know? Oh yes you do, I was the only one English boy in the course because all of the boys were the different Ethnic like Chinese, Indian etc. The 3 girls kept following me, the girls were about the same age as me and they liked me a lot; we had our meals together. I have been surrounded by them for 24 hours and in the evening it was nice and warm, and we went out for a walk by the canal, chatting and giggling, then we stopped at the pub near the hostel on the way back for a drink and had a chat. It was a nice pub with street lights along the River Thames when it was getting dark, the girls have been mucking about with me all night along, we stayed there until 11pm after the others went back to the hostel. In the whole group we were the last people to go to bed because afterwards we went in hostel bar relaxing in the lounge sofa together, we even played cushion fight there before we went to bed!

The weekend has been great fun and I passed the First Aid. At the end all of the girls asked for my phone number; they don't live too far from me which I thought was great because I never had some friends like them. One of the girls has a cochlear implant same as me but she has a different make; she was the youngest in the course as she is 16; – really nice, she was full of fun.

I am continuing to stay with FYD and hope to go on ACD course (Action Centred Development) which is one year long with 2 day Training every 2 months to develop skills for further education or employment and to be more confident in myself.

Now I will move on. My college is going well and I don't have to stick to my timetables, I can come as I please because the great news is I have passed my exam that I failed last January. I have been gaining quite a lot of good grades so far, also I am allowed to leave any time when all my assignments are completed. I hoped I would leave in the end of May but it was too much work and hard because am not enjoying developing a program because I have to learn the computer language and how to write the program, so I hope to leave this week hopefully. My best part of the course is doing graphic design on computer because I like to be creative and practical, my lecturers have always praised me for brilliant designs. They have asked me to think about doing CAD (Computer Aided Design) course after this and I have considered doing this. I am hoping to go to London College of Printing to do CAD course on computer, as a part-time course because I am going to be a trainee at my dad's printing firm in Dartford. In the family I am now the computer whizz; I am always on stand by for my mum when she does typing on the computer!

Travelling to Croydon can be a pain because of the Tram road works; one morning going to college took me one and half hours to get there, a real nightmare. Apart from the nightmare sometimes life there is OK, the BBC 'The Bill' came to film outside the college for their programme but I don't know when it will be screened on TV.

Change of subject, I am not sure if you knew that the chinchillas had 2 babies last July, so this year same thing happened this May half term by giving birth to THREE babies. They looked so cute, 2 of them were light grey and other dark, one of the babies was so active and kept running about, climbing a lot and this one was the one who kept escaping from the cage. I was the first person to the rescue scooping the baby from the floor, it was so light as a paper and cud-

dly, fluffy and by the time I put my hand in the cage the baby wouldn't leave my hand, but one week later the other one has died. Now the other two are all well and are growing a lot.

My brother Dan is nearly finishing his 3 years course at Brighton Uni and he is waiting to hear if he gets a degree in Graphic Design and it would be a great joy to have him back as my good old brother. Dan is going to Australia this November for a month with his girlfriend to Perth.

I am quite busy every Monday going to work at St. George's Player's drama group after college doing painting preparing for this July Two One Act plays starting on 4th July, I am enjoying it and the manager gets a great advantage of me being there.

Thanks for the birthday card, I had Kickers jumper and T-shirt, some money also Learn to Drive video for the deaf with Text, this summer I hope that Dan and I will be buying a car together and learn to drive and at the moment I am learning theory test.

On 11th May, I walked gruelling 16 miles over all London bridges to raise money for the Aid of The National Kidney foundation with my mum and her friend starting at Battersea Park all way over the bridges that leads to London Tower then walked reverse back to Battersea Park, with 500 other people, it took us 5 hours with only 20 minutes lunch break. It was very aching work, the wind was unbelievable when I walked over the bridges, so windy and it rained for some periods. We raised £160 altogether, and 50% of the money goes towards Bromley Chain charity for the Deaf.

That's all for me to say, Cheerio and good luck in future and see you when you are back here. Love from Thomas.

A Chance to be Heard

So many hearing people equate poor speech or a reticence to use voice with a lack of language and, by implication, intelligence. Equally, oral deaf lip-readers with intelligible speech can often 'talk the hind leg off a donkey' but frequently commandeer the conversation in order that they don't have to try and concentrate to fathom out what anyone else might want to say. Tom is certainly never guilty of that but he has a great desire to communicate and, with hearing people who don't understand signing, letters or emails are the only way he can do so. Their inclusion here gives Tom's 'voice' a chance to be heard and his personality to permeate pages where hitherto it's been me doing most of the talking. His writing, which he uses to impart information, to thank, to cajole, to commiserate, to comment, to explain, to negotiate and to tease could possibly make the case for (or against, if the reader is so minded) the use of Signed English and SSE with a young deaf child.

In this technological age it sometimes feels as if the art of letter writing is likely to be lost. But if a deaf youngster can put pen to paper and write letters like these, while still of course enjoying emails as much as anyone of his generation, I think there is hope for us yet!

Chapter 12

Borneo and Beyond

Life is either a daring adventure or nothing (Helen Keller)

In July 1999 a hearing friend, David Rose, treasurer on Bromley Chain committee, decided to take up the Trans-Borneo Cycle Challenge 2000 for Sense (The National Deafblind and Rubella Association). I knew it was something Tom would dearly love to do and without too much persuasion he too duly applied and paid the deposit. It was to take place in April 2000 so he had nine months in which to raise the required minimum of £2000 sponsorship. I imagined it would probably be very difficult but I had reckoned without our friends at St George's and others in the community. First to sign up were Jackie and Susie, his teachers from the unit days, quickly followed by local friends. Because Tom had helped design posters for a flower festival and had worked on the souvenir brochure which I wrote and Froude Printing produced, Elizabeth and Jean, the 'flower ladies' at church, put on a tropicana evening to help boost his fund-raising. On a dark February night the transformation of the church hall into a tropical paradise with palm trees on a sandy 'island' and amazing table decorations of exotica, was the most heart-warming sight, to say nothing of the delicious food and all the love that had gone into the preparations. Tom's own bike and helmet were on display as well as a map of Borneo with the route picked out in felt pen and a board showing all the hints and reminders we had gleaned from a Sense briefing at the British Medical Association when the previous year's cyclists had told it like it was! And, to our delight, Tom's old friend Caroline had flown in from Australia just hours before and was able to join us.

Yvonne, a friend from National Childbirth Trust days who first met Tom as a baby shortly before her first child was born, asked the head teacher of the local Roman Catholic primary school where she is a teacher if her class could run a raffle for Tom. In the end it was not just her class but the entire school which took part, and the generosity of the parents and children in providing raffle prizes was truly amazing; three tables groaned under the weight of prizes! Tom bashfully accepted the invitation to attend the special assembly which coincided with the week during which my colour photograph and news story about him had graced the front page of the local free newspaper, *The Leader*. He was thus, in the eyes of the children, something of a celebrity, with his picture on the notice boards and a huge 'Welcome to St Mary's, Tom' in the hall. Everyone, it's been said, has their 15 minutes of fame, but his lasted far longer than that as the winning tickets were drawn, and drawn, and drawn . . . This generosity resulted in £302 for the charity Sense and every child in class 1F had made him a card with a message. My favourite one said 'I hope you have enof [sic] money' and each one brought home to me just how difficult it is to draw a bicycle!

I sent off a feature for the Mothers' Union magazine *Home and Family* and was over the moon when the editor, Jill Worth, wanted not only to print it but also to have some more information and photographs added to it. I offered to give my talk 'Signs and wonders' to any group willing to make a small donation to Sense and, as a result, I went as far as Rochester to speak, as well as receiving cheques from interested readers, including one Jenny Froude from Surrey. And I had always thought I was unique! Our parish magazine carried my article about Tom's plans and members of the congregation were so supportive, pressing money into my hands for the cause rather than my having to target too many people with a sponsorship form. Tom himself did sponsored car-cleaning and some computer advice to a deaf friend also resulted in a donation. St George's Players generously allowed him a share of their annual pantomime raffle, which took place while he was beavering away behind scenes with curtains, props and other paraphernalia. I probably 'bored for England' with talks to local groups such as Soroptimist International, Probus Club, Catholic Women's League, Afternoon Women's Fellowship and a Social Services special needs evening. Apart from anything else, these talks were a good way of raising Deaf Awareness in the community and the response was heart-warming. My 'It makes sense to be sixty' birthday lunch when I asked for donations to 'Sense' rather than presents to me swelled the coffers by over £400. I felt proud of Tom and humbled by the response to his appeal from both the deaf and hearing communities.

Tom joined the local gym and started going regularly, and swimming, although he didn't find time to do many long cycle rides which worried me. He and Dan did cycle to Brighton one Sunday but I was rather shaken to find it had taken them hours to arrive and they reached there at 6 p.m. rather than lunchtime as I'd fondly imagined! Doubts began to set in as to whether Tom would stay the course . . .

In December John retired and Tom was far from happy. Communication was very difficult once he was without anyone able or willing to understand him at the printing company and in January he faxed his resignation, without telling us of his plans, and took off for the day to think things through. I explained that we supported his decision but that he had gone about it in quite the wrong way.

Tom was able to survive on his savings while he concentrated on training for the cycle challenge. There was a prodigious amount of expensive equipment to buy or borrow, from special padded Lycra shorts, wicking tee shirts and socks, anti mosquito sprays and nets, high factor sun screens, buffs (brilliant seamless tube of jersey fabric which can be worn dampened round the neck or head to protect from the sun and help keep cool) enormous containers of electrolyte powders and water bottles, malaria tablets and energy bars.

Having seen the exorbitant cost of the latter I decided to buy a few and make the remainder. Using the Neal's Yard (Covent Garden) bakery book I dutifully mixed nuts, honey, molasses, oats and other nutritious items into a batch of bars which met with his approval. I wrapped each in silver foil and placed them in a zipped polythene bag, only to be informed by Dan that on an airport X-ray machine they would probably look exactly like illegal substances! Given that Tom's dear friend Edna, a churchwarden, had designed her own card for him innocently saying 'Keep peddling [sic] Tom – we are all behind you, pushing!' I thought we could all be in hot water! As it happened the energy bars found their way back to England in the bottom of his luggage. He said he couldn't fancy anything other than fresh, juicy pineapples when he was cycling, but the bars were not wasted. They gave me the energy I needed to tackle all the dirty washing that spewed out of his backpack a few days after his return!

Final Preparations

After all the months of planning and fund-raising, the day before departure seemed to dawn quite suddenly. At that time St George's was bracing itself for the inevitable death of one of the most loved and admired of men. Steffen Conway, who as lay reader had prepared all three of our sons for their Confirmation, was diagnosed with inoperable pancreatic cancer in November 1998. He was then in the middle of training for the non-stipendiary ministry and in September 1999 he was ordained priest by the Bishop of Tonbridge in a special service at St George's. I knew he would be celebrating the Wednesday morning Eucharist on 12 April and Tom agreed to come with me; Father Steffen had promised him a good send off.

It was an especially memorable service, for so many reasons. Jenny, a dear friend from my time as her volunteer at St Christopher's Hospice, still reeling from the shock of her post as Chaplain's PA being made redundant, was there, and Tessa, a teacher, ex-Youth Club leader and great friend, who has always been incredibly supportive of all three of our sons. Afterwards, over coffee in the glassed-off narthex area at the back of church, Steffen told those who didn't already know what Tom was about to undertake and, despite his own extreme frailty, remembered and quoted all the inconsequential things I had just told him about the preparations and packing. The few photographs I took then are particularly precious – of a man in his fifties and a boy of twenty, both of them embarking on journeys into the unknown. Poignantly, exactly one month after his departure, Tom was back with us at Steffen's funeral, at which I had the bittersweet privilege of reading the poem 'The seated celebrant' I had been moved to write earlier in the year.

Knowing that Tom's first day of the Challenge would see him cycling from 0 to 6500 feet, I stuck a copy of Psalm 121 in his good luck card (showing a bowler hatted man on a tandem with a female, whose figure, hair style, specs and sweater were not unlike my own, seated behind him with arms folded and legs parallel to the ground) in which I said I'd be behind him all the way!

> 'I lift up my eyes to the hills – where does my help come from?
> My help comes from the Lord, the Maker of heaven and earth.
> He will not let your foot slip – he who watches over you will not slumber;
> Indeed, he who watches over Israel will neither slumber nor sleep.
> The Lord watches over you – the Lord is your shade at your right hand
> The sun will not harm you by day, nor the moon by night.
> The Lord will keep you from all harm – he will watch over your life;
> The Lord will watch over your coming and going both now and for evermore'.

Diary Detail

Tom's experiences of Borneo formed part of a 19-page email diary which he sent in instalments to any friends who had expressed an interest. It became an ongoing saga which was not completed until nine months after the event and it makes breathless reading. Partly because, in his enthusiasm to commit all his experiences to paper, I guess Tom forgot all he ever learnt about punctuation but mainly because it is so evocative that one feels one's almost sweating up those hills, in that intense heat and humidity, with him. Despite a passion for proof-reading, about which I'm frequently teased, I would not presume to touch a word of it; this is *his* record of *his* adventure and the fact that he wanted to set it down in such detail on screen and paper was all that mattered to me.

Taking a break on Mt. Kinabalu

The trip obviously meant such a lot to him, not only for the sense of achievement

> *my proudest moment was when, having completed the morning cycle on a good surface, then tough off road cycling after lunch, only eight out of thirty cyclists, including me, opted to cycle the last part, mostly off-road on a very rough, hilly road on such a hot afternoon, before reaching Ranau where it ended*

but for the camaraderie it engendered. 'Everyone in the group has been wonderful and so friendly that they have even wanted to learn to sign so we could socialise in the evenings'. Maybe it's something of regret that it takes a gruelling team event to get hearing people to accept deaf people and meet them half way but if that's the case, Tom will go for it!

John Hurd, one of the recipients of the diary, emailed later:

> Tom's accounts of his joys and sufferings in Borneo made a good read. Quite the Hero – I'd have chucked it at the first touch of discomfort; must admire his grit. It was such a good read I forgot he shouldn't have that level of insight and language.

Appreciative comments from someone who had, in his own inimitable way, been instrumental in aiding both those aspects of Tom's development.

The cyclists covered 225 miles in the six days after they rode out of Kota Kinabalu with, to Tom's delight, a police escort, and the average tempera-

The Sense Cycle Challenge comes to an end at Sandakan (Tom is 2nd from left, front row)

ture was 40 degrees, 100% humidity. Heat exhaustion, dehydration and sunstroke were very real dangers, about which they had been well warned by Sense back in England, and there were times when the cyclists had to take a break and recover in the air-conditioned back-up coach. Thomas raised around £4500 in sponsorship and I know he would do it all again if only it were possible! The months of planning and preparation seemed to drag; the event itself seemed to be over far too quickly for him and he wrote, as they finished on a damp, hazy day at the Buddhist temple at Sandakan that he felt 'happiness and sadness' and wished it could last longer.

Due to the late Easter that year, David and Tom's plans to stay on in Borneo for a few days' holiday did not materialise as flight alterations proved impossible to make. As it happened, it was probably just as well since he came home in a sorry state on Easter Sunday.

We were all waiting in the arrival area at Heathrow Airport, convincing ourselves that every tall male looming into view was bound to be Tom, but again and again being disappointed. Eventually we spotted David with a luggage trolley but where, oh where, was that tall person who should be with him? And then we saw him! Sitting shamefaced in a wheelchair was Tom. I imagined a broken leg until I caught sight of his feet. Believe me, size eleven feet, swollen from a long flight and badly burnt, are not a pretty sight! The poor kid had fallen asleep on the beach on the last day (exhausted no doubt after all the energy expenditure) and they had

Tom and David safely back in Bromley after their exertions in the wilds of Borneo

suffered burns which had been exacerbated by the swelling on the flight. An ignominious homecoming for our hero. For at least a week he could hardly walk and after two days had to hobble barefoot into the doctor's surgery to show him the blisters that had appeared. Fortunately they did not burst or become infected and by the following week he could once again bear to put on some shoes. Until then I told him it must be God's way of making sure he rested and regained some energy after all his exertions! Looking back at the homecoming photographs some months later I realised how gaunt and haggard he appeared but it was not until I 'overheard' him signing to a deaf committee member that he had lost a stone in Borneo that I realised why. He should have eaten those energy bars after all! I am not sure if he hadn't confessed his weight loss to me because he knew I'd be worried or, more likely, very envious.

A few months later a small group of the intrepid cyclists had a reunion and cycled to Hever Castle in Kent, stopping in the rain *en route* for some pineapple thoughtfully provided by Diane, one of the two other deaf cyclists. I doubt it tasted half as good as the Malaysian version.

Future Plans

After his return from Borneo, Tom was busy with three other deaf friends setting up a much-needed deaf social club in the Bromley area. On the work front he took a temporary stop-gap job as a cleaner in Holmes Sports Club, the only snag being that he started at 5.30 in the morning. That summer he had news of what sounded a marvellous opportunity specifically for disabled people, of an apprenticeship scheme at the Royal Opera House. He applied with high hopes but, alas, was not short-listed for an interview. No doubt with a brief of any age, any disability, there were very many excellent applicants from which to choose.

At his own instigation, while deciding what his future career plans would be, he had an interview for Tesco Direct Internet Home Shopping Service and was called for a second one a few weeks later, after which he was told he could start in December 2000. He had two weeks' signing help from David, his companion in Borneo who was by then working for Deaf Umbrella, a communication support service, and quickly picked up the routine. He has been there for two years and is enjoying being part of what seems to be a very supportive team. One area of concern was the fire alarm and since, because of the design of the building, vibrating pagers would not work, a system of mentors was set up to alert him. This was put to the test in a genuine incident when the rotisserie caught fire and the store was evacuated. It seems not just one but all members of his team located him; he himself had heard a new sound but not realised what it was. He came home and described the whole event to me as a 'high drama' and laughed when I asked him where he got such language! Even in his twenties he still has the power to make me delight in what he signs / says; I still don't take anything for granted and I doubt I ever shall.

Chapter 13

What Is Deaf?

> Not our song but our silence passes all understanding.
> And we are silent when we sing. (Mark Roper, 1997).

'Please, what is *deaf*?' Many years ago, this perfectly natural query from my friend's puzzled foreign au pair set me thinking. How does one describe an invisible handicap? What was it that set my four-year-old son apart from her four-year-old charge? On the surface, not a lot. Both were robust and extrovert. Both were even named Thomas! But *my* Thomas didn't turn when I called him. The noise of the traffic was meaningless to him. He didn't hear the silly asides the other boys laughed at in the car *en route* to their weekly swimming class. But once he was there, he was one of the lads – first across the width, first on the float, first to relinquish his arm-bands. He lip-read, he copied, he had been used to the school situation since he was three years old, and already had a confidence and maturity that many of his age could envy. He related well to other people, adored babies, was very caring towards everyone. He was a vital part of our family, of his nursery class, of our local and church community. The fact that his ears no longer worked did not make him stupid. He used his eyes to give him a lot of the information he needed, and his hands to convey it to the few others who understood sign.

His vocabulary increased each day. Of course he could not hear my shouted warning (or the odd swear word when the going got tough)! He missed out on all the information hearing children pick up, much of it subconsciously, throughout the day. His understanding could never be smugly assumed; we had to check again and again that he had really understood. And when a child is deaf he has to come searching for you; it's no use you shouting to him to tell him you're only in the loo! If you want *him* you have physically to go and locate him: no bellowing up the stairs, down the garden or across the playground! All this becomes second nature very quickly and it is only when describing the situation to another (or on the Disability Living Allowance forms) that one realises just how time-consuming many daily exchanges actually become.

'Look at me when I'm talking to you' – luckily never a problem with Tom!

I quickly discovered that it is impossible to sign and do anything else at the same time. With a hearing child one can toss a remark over the shoulder, call from another room, carry on a conversation while cooking, washing-up, writing, typing, phoning, sewing, knitting, eating, drinking. Two hands are needed for signing so every other activity must stop. In order to be lip-read, the speaker must be positioned so that the deaf person can see him or her clearly, with the light falling on the face rather than with the back to the window. Lighting must be good. A dark winter night and a protracted power cut made me wonder how deaf people coped in the days before electricity. I was blinded by having a torch shone in my face every time Tom wanted to lip-read me! No doubt candles made a kinder option, despite the shadows they cast.

Outside the home, even walking along the road and trying to sign or lip-read can cause unwelcome contact with obstacles such as lamp-posts, or even other pedestrians, in mid-conversation. All dialogue has to be one-to-one and face-to-face in the case of a profoundly deaf person. If one is absolutely honest, there have got to be times when silence is no longer golden.

By virtue of the white stick, blind people quite rightly command attention and offers of assistance. A hearing aid invokes no such sympathetic response; people simply regard it as a preserve of the elderly. They do not expect to see one worn by a child. The sight of two-year-old Tom's led to a friendly overture from an old man on the bus one day. He pointed to his own hearing aid and commiserated with Tom. 'I know just how you feel, old son!' But of course the irony was, he didn't, having become deaf late in life, after years of normal hearing had given him all he needed in the way of speech and language. His deafness was probably no more than an irritation to him, not something that had coloured his entire life.

Another occasion springs to mind when Tom's youth belied his disability. Visiting his cousins in Hastings when he was about two years old he fell heavily in the garden and seemed in such distress we took him to casualty late in the evening. Exhausted by his tears he had slumped asleep against my shoulder, dislodging his hearing aid which, of course, launched into the familiar whistle which never ceased to have the ladies in our local post office on red alert! Loath to disturb him I let it continue and we arrived in the busy waiting room.

'What's that noise?' demanded a middle-aged lady. Her friend supplied the answer. 'That's a hearing aid. I know because Uncle Harry used to have one that made that noise. Nearly drove us mad!' With that their eyes scanned the waiting room searching for the sound source. When they spotted a poor old man with a huge bump on his head and a suitably hangdog expression he became the focus of their attention and accusing glances. Satisfied that they had identified the culprit they never dreamed for a moment that our small mite was the offender! Worried about Tom as I was I felt in no mood to enlighten them, although I suspect they must have realised once we were summoned for an X-ray and the whistling ceased with our departure.

Deaf Awareness

Deafness went undetected on that occasion. However, I think we mums of deaf children recognise each other. When Tom was two we took him to Howlett's Zoo in Kent. Standing watching a family of elephants I heard a voice behind me exclaim 'Oh look, there's a *baby* one!' The intonation was so like my own I swung round, convinced I'd see a mum with a deaf child. But no, the child with the speaker had no hearing aid. Later, however, I had to retrace my steps and passed the same woman and this time I could see she had a child in a pushchair with her. And, yes, that child was wearing a Phonic Ear radio aid. I *was* right after all! We mums sound alike and small wonder we are renowned for suffering from verbal diarrhoea! Our children don't overhear information and so points need to be stressed, over and over again. What's more, because we have to feed them so much information, it's all too easy to impart our own prejudices or hang-ups. I feel we have to be very careful of this awesome responsibility we have in interpreting some situations for them.

If you hear nothing, not even your own voice, then it is obviously impossible to monitor it. Some deaf people have loud voices, some very strained ones, many have unintelligible ones. It is all too easy for a listener unused to deaf voices to assume that their sounds signal a lack of intelligence as well as of hearing. The label 'deaf-and-dumb' is the most hurtful of all, of course, since the word dumb today has connotations of stupidity. I have heard a headteacher in school refer to the 'deafos' in the unit and that, arguably, was more unforgivable than the remark made by a man watching the Bromley Chain float pass by in the carnival procession. He watched the deaf children communicating excitedly with each other and with the onlookers and then, brushing the collecting bucket aside, said 'Oh look, *they're* not deaf! What a fiddle!'

There are other unintentional hurts as well. The mother who commented gleefully 'I guess we have Tom to thank for X getting a place at Clare House school'. And very likely they did, since the over-subscribed school was opposite our house and they were not in the catchment area. But I didn't want reminding of the fact that yet another of our three sons was denied the chance of attending the highly-thought-of school we'd watched being built right on our doorstep. And the mother who was seeking commiseration for her son who was having to start wearing spectacles, 'poor little thing'– I couldn't help feeling that body-worn hearing aids on a three-year-old were far more incongruous and the reason for wearing them far more serious. Depending on how things were going or my mood at the time it was possible to either laugh such thoughtless remarks off or to take them to heart.

Aids to Living

In adulthood, profound deafness means the need for an interpreter, a lip-speaker or a note-taker to provide equal access to meetings, interviews, lectures, seminars and so on. Also, probably for medical or dental appointments, for parents' evenings at school, for legal or religious events. It means the use of flashing light doorbells and other alerting devices, vibrating pagers, alarm clocks and smoke alarms. It means there is a need for text telephones, the services of Typetalk telephone relay system, fax machines, access to the World Wide Web and the Internet. In order to be able to understand television programmes subtitles are essential and Teletext pages to provide extra information. A special video recorder is needed to record subtitled programmes and a decoder is required to access closed captioned video films. Modern technology that benefits the hearing world, in particular mobile phone text messages, as well as visual displays on railway stations, trains and at some bus stops are a huge step forward for deaf people, too.

Yes, the technology is certainly there in this new century *but* none of these things should be a substitute for the *personal* touch. I often think that if well-meaning people didn't always insist on having something *tangible* to donate to a deaf child or adult, if they themselves were willing to take time to learn how to communicate in some way, by learning to sign or speaking clearly, that could well be a more valuable investment than all the latest equipment. All too often deaf people are let down by the attitudes of hearing people. These may be born of impatience (because it takes longer to attract deaf people's attention, to explain things, to understand them) or of embarrassment (due to *their* difficult speech or *our* inability to sign, and an ever present fear of being misunderstood) or, more likely, of blissful ignorance. But hearing people can, and do, so easily turn deafness into a very real handicap for those who live with it all day, every day.

Tom himself put the importance of *people* very firmly in perspective for me when he was 11 years old. He had been brought home ill from school and found me there alone. He obviously thought about the implications of that and asked, 'Are you lonely here all day when me and Dan and Matt are away?' 'No', I replied, 'not really, because I have so many things to do'. Tom looked at me rather witheringly and said, with great perception, 'Yes, but *things* aren't *people!*' So often it was not only his deafness that was profound . . .

Deafness, then, is more than a lack of hearing. It is a whole way of life. In some instances it is a whole different culture with its own language (British Sign Language), its own clubs, its own magazines, its own humour, its own Deaf pride. At 22 years Tom is now part of that – but he is also very much part of the hearing world too, in as much as he enjoys the company of his hearing friends, reads and writes well, is interested in everything and actively wants to hear things. I think he is therefore deaf with a small 'd' since he uses SSE (Sign Supported English) rather than BSL most of the time. Users of the latter are deaf with a capital D and there can, at times, be a whole big gulf between the two. A totally deaf friend, who lost his hearing some 40-odd years ago, is referred to by the Deaf community as simply 'hard of hearing'. Why? Because he has retained his strong, 'normal' voice, and relies on lip-reading rather than signing. Other Deaf people may have had an oral upbringing and only embraced the Deaf community in adulthood. They now campaign vocif-

People have always been important to Tom. He
is enchanted by his Deaf friends' baby, Marcus

erously for the use of BSL but seem to conveniently forget that it was the
exposure to English which has given them the means to do so in a literate
and therefore beneficial way. Again I have to agree with Tom Bertling
that 'to disregard or diminish the language of the rest of our society
cannot possibly benefit our deaf children'.

'Deaf people don't make pretty speeches', said one Deaf friend to me,
quite proudly one day. Perhaps she had no idea how much a 'pretty speech'
as she called it can do to oil the wheels of communication. Being blunt and
to the point and not taking other people's feelings into account is not the
best way to endear oneself. Tom's language has always reflected this subtle
sensitivity, I'm glad to say, as witness his query to me after my mother died,
and his letters to the ailing Roy Castle and Wendy after the bereavements
she suffered. It's the part of Tom's personality in which I take most
pleasure, and maybe just a little motherly pride.

The politics of deafness are much to the fore in this new millennium. I wonder what I would say now to that enquiring young au pair – and what she would make of Tom's progress in the world since the time she first wondered at his deafness and what it meant.

Chapter 14

Paths to Understanding

I'm worth all the time it takes to understand me. (Charles Schulz)

These words appear on a pint-sized 'Peanuts' T-shirt which Tom wore as a toddler. The slogan is as apt today as it was all those years ago, when I tried to put myself in his shoes and anticipate what he might need, or think, delight in or worry about, find confusing or incomprehensible. It need not be only the prerogative of *deaf* parents to empathise with a deaf child; given the confidence we others can be equally sensitive to their needs.

Hearing parents are reputed to despair, after diagnosis, that their deaf infant will never be able to say 'I love you' to them. That was never my concern. Mine was that Tom would never hear *us* say we loved *him*. Maybe that subtle shift of emphasis accounts for much of our relationship. And now the tables are very healthily turned and it is Tom who puts himself in *my* shoes. He sends my emails for me, guides me through the things that baffle me on the computer by composing simplified operating instructions that even an idiot mother can comprehend, and patiently feeds paper into a problematic printer. In more ways than one, it is certainly true to say that without him this book would not have been written!

Given the chance to delete or amend anything contained within these pages Tom found nothing he wished to alter but said simply 'It's very good for my Memory Lane!' He has always had a delightfully individual way with words. His fairly recently coined 'godmacked' somehow sounds so much nicer than the horrid 'gobsmacked' on which it was based. But it was in one of his early letters – I believe to the BBC children's television programme Blue Peter – that he endearingly added, in brackets beneath his signature 'proudly found deaf'. Of all his 'Froudian' slips that is the one I treasure most!

And I treasured so much over the years, as will be obvious by this celebration of his life so far. It's a celebration in the main of the *small* things – or at any rate things that may well seem to be small to those for whom life has been all plain sailing – but which for us often represent a huge amount of effort. If his was a big 'success story' in the eyes of today's world his speech

Surprise guest in confident dialogue with Jackie Parsons at her leaving party, July 2002

by now would have, against all the odds, been honed to sweetest clarity. He would have taken A-levels, gone to university, have a wide circle of deaf and hearing friends. He would even have been on the way to the first Ferrari by now!

But what he *has* done is to have proved himself in areas too many to mention. He has stayed true to himself. He has always been willing to 'have a go'. His confidence, which was shaken in school Year 9, is taking a long time to return. He has coped and come through epilepsy and migraine, with a late cochlear implant that initially didn't go according to plan, and with a gruelling challenge in the wilds of Borneo. And, without being smug, but simply sincerely grateful for the right suggestions at the right time, I think the key to his development has been communication. For us total communication has worked!

A lot of the things I did in the early days were born of my own 'gut' feeling, allied to the good advice we were given. It's comforting now to read respected writers confirm that the road we chose was a sound one.

> Immature personalities of many pre-verbally deaf children are the re-
> sult of poor early parent–child relationships and the child's lack of an

effective means of communication in the early formative years. John C. Denmark (1994).

And Marschark (1997) writes that 'Early language experience for deaf children has been shown to have a significant impact on their personalities and emotional development, just as it does with hearing children'. He feels 'the important thing is to have consistent two-way communication, regardless of whether it is spoken or signed' and I am sure he is right. But much must depend, I feel, on the degree of hearing loss and for Tom I am still certain signing was the very best option.

Identity Issues

Of course there have been some difficult moments. Tom said in an interview that he was seven before he realised he was deaf but, checking back, I see he was identifying with a deaf boy on television as early as five years of age. 'Deaf, same as me and Brett and Mark' he had said/signed quite matter-of-factly, and he referred to himself that same spring as a 'deaf Easter rabbit!'

By the time he was in his teens he was writing in true adolescent angst 'I hate myself. I hate my face' but with the added poignancy 'I don't like to be deaf'. In his Transition Statement, compiled before the cochlear implant, he wrote 'sometimes I hate myself for being deaf. It is like being locked in cells with no sounds', but I have to admit that, even at the time, I felt it was more of a dramatic comment bandied around and seized upon by the unit group rather than his truly individual response.

I know deaf youngsters are likely to be influenced by their teachers and peers but outside this realm I had not expected to have the infuriating experience of seeing 12-year-old Tom being assailed by a deaf adult trying to get him to admit to feelings of anger and frustration because, she implied, all deaf people in hearing families have those feelings deep inside them. Slumped in a chair after an exhausting day at school, somewhat bewildered by the diatribe which appeared to have been provoked by the innocent enquiry of another visitor, Tom put up very little resistance to the notion. But he confessed to me when we were alone later that he didn't really share those feelings at all! Unlike some, I'm sure, he certainly had very little reason for feeling deprived or misunderstood, but I felt angry that he'd been subjected to what I saw as a mild form of brainwashing. At times I have felt that good relationships at home in a hearing family are seen as a threat by a few in the Deaf community who seem, in a perverse and maybe patriarchal way, to expect and prefer us to fail. Tom himself is the first to admit he has been fortunate in so many ways, not least in having communication at home from babyhood and in being allowed and supported with the desired cochlear implant in his teens.

I have always hated comparisons. It doesn't do to compare child with child, adult with adult, and one certainly should not, and cannot, compare deaf with deaf. Even the term profoundly deaf can cover a whole range of ability. Depending in which frequencies the useful parts of hearing occur, reliance on lip-reading alone and production of intelligible speech is possible. How often have I heard brilliant percussionist Evelyn Glennie cited as an example to deaf people; many expect them all to be as vocal and as musical as she is! Likewise, all implanted people will do differently; there can be no hard and fast expectations or outcomes. Families too will vary. Every family of a deaf youngster has different priorities, social or cultural pressures, needs, hopes, fears, experiences and aspirations.

I'd imagined I couldn't cope with another child with special needs, but when I had to it became a joy as well as a challenge. The fact that Tom has turned out an independent, well-rounded personality, with a compassion for others, a sense of humour, a willingness to consider opposing view-points and always ready to accept a challenge is a blessing almost too big to believe!

At one time I thought his first few weeks and the precious notes I entrusted to the back of a diary in hospital, and which form part of Chapter 1, would be all we had to remember him by. Every August I count our blessings, realising that we could so easily be listening out for his name to be read in church on a list of the departed 'whose anniversaries occur at this time' and I say a prayer of thanksgiving and ask anew for a blessing on all the medical staff who worked so compassionately to save his life.

Even now there are times when I wish I had been the sort of parent who phones for help at the slightest provocation. Sometimes I am haunted by the thought that Tom might have stayed unscathed if I'd called the doctor earlier, but then I wonder if, instead, a locum might have arrived, it being Bank Holiday, and simply given him a baby medicine which could have clouded the issue and led to his death. We shall never know.

There are also times when I think I may have accepted the deafness too comfortably. Have I sometimes felt *my* importance magnified as a result of *his* hearing loss? I hope not, since it is, after all, Tom's life and he has to live with it and the limitations it sometimes imposes in communication, in socialising, in studying, in job satisfaction, in day-to-day living.

Speech and Language

Although I know I suffer from an ostrich-like tendency to bury my head in the sand, I am all too aware that the discrepancy between Tom's command of language and the quality of his speech is the thing that pains him more than anything else. And because it does it can't help but distress me, too. I also know that it must hurt him when, usually due to tiredness, I haven't been able to understand him. That's when I feel a thoughtless failure, just as I did when Tom caught me tapping my foot to a Cliff Richard tune on the television. He was only 11 years old at the time but when I queried his melancholy expression he gave me an old-fashioned look and said 'You know what I'm thinking', adding rather bashfully, 'I want to hear'. And, yes, I did know he wanted to hear and it was the one thing not in my power to give him. We mums have special gifts, maybe, but they are not always the ones we most want or need.

I am well aware that we have been very lucky in Tom and that not all experiences are as positive as ours, for whatever reason. If I have painted what some might see as a misleadingly rosy picture, I can only apologise. This is simply a story born of *our* experience, some aspects of which will be common to all parents, others ours alone. What I do hope is that I have been able to capture something of Tom in these pages so that his character comes across. I would like to think that his story, which having planned to write when he was three years old I determined to finish by his twenty-first birthday, may give a small insight into the nature of profound deafness to those who have no experience of it, and a feeling of hope and a smattering of knowledge to those who are now, or may be in the future, inescapably involved with it. And, above all, I hope this book has not read like one of those cringe-making, mass-produced, self-congratulatory missives that fall through the letter-box at Christmas, extolling the virtues and cata-loguing the achievements of every youngster in the family. That was never my intention!

Such Special Support

Our older sons, Matthew and Daniel, may not have been mentioned very frequently in these pages but they know, and we know, that without them Tom's story would not have been the rich one it is. They are no less precious and we are no less proud of them; this is as much their story as Tom's, since they have played such a huge part in making our family life what it is. Looking back I can see how easy it would have been for them to have resented the extra time Tom took and to have rebelled against him and against us. Instead they have stayed quietly supportive, justifiably proud of him and, simply by their very presence, have put things in perspective. Like John, their father, to whom I have been happily married for 40 years, and who, I'm sure, would be the first to admit has never been the world's best communicator, their dependable love has given me a strength and

At the centre of a supportive family – Tom on our Ruby Wedding Anniversary, June 2002

stability I've been able to rely on. That, allied to the faith I have been blessed with, has been all I have needed.

Blindness, it is acknowledged, cuts one off from *things*; deafness cuts one off from *people*. The hearing wax lyrical about birdsong and Beethoven and try to imagine life without either. But, spurning such sentiment, surely there other more important factors at stake – such as hearing your siblings and friends call you, your father warn you of danger, your mother and, later, your partner whisper terms of endearment? Despite not being able to enjoy those things that we take for granted, I hope that nothing in our family life cut Tom off from us and, although it has been all too easy to go into a time warp during the happy recall of bygone years, I feel fairly confident that those early days still stand us in good stead. Even if it is sometimes difficult to reconcile that tiny Tom with the lanky version that prowls round the work station and reminds me that it's time for supper!

At one of the early Nuffield courses at Ealing we were told that with a deaf child 'you get back what you put in' but our experience has been oh so much more than that. The extra dimension Tom has given to our lives is incalculable. The challenge of a deaf child is immense; the rewards in our case have far outweighed the worries. Our miracle was that, thanks to so many prayers from so many people, Thomas survived what could have been fatal meningitis. Since that first, dreadful August day, people have come into our lives whose skill and support have helped us survive and cope, firstly with the illness, and secondly with its legacy.

'God bless my lovely Mr Hurd', signed/said a small Tom many years ago.

And still today I add a heartfelt 'Amen' to that.

Appendix 1

**A Letter to a Deaf Son 'Yellow is a Lovely Word to See'
(written in Spring 1981, more in joy than in sorrow, but above
all, in hope)**

We have a lot to learn, you and I

Not for us the joy of nonsensical verbal banter – my speech must in the main be meaningful to you.

Some of our play must be 'contrived', structured to help you understand language. You must learn to listen, your hearing aid isn't open sesame to speech as some would like to believe. Sources of sound must be pointed out to you, over and over again.

You must be 'conditioned' (such a horrible word) to wait for noise and act accordingly so that you can one day be given an audiogram to chart what remains of your hearing.

My face must be watched for clues. (I wish it were a comely one for your close scrutiny!)

You will have to study my lips to 'see' words, hence my title.

My hands might one day have to make specific signs for you. I hope they will be expressively eloquent for you.

My presence will be important to you, but let me not mollycoddle you, make you too dependent, or curb your natural wanderlust.

We have a lot to discover, you and I

Your head doesn't turn at my footstep nor yet at my voice. I must remember not to come upon you suddenly and startle you.

It comes naturally to touch you to attract your attention but, if this becomes a habit, you might copy and other children might resent it, not understanding . . .

You may never *hear* us say we love you but I hope you won't need words to tell you how much we care. Your other senses are already so acute.

167

We have a lot to remember, you and I

I must remember not to become so preoccupied with decibels and frequencies, with the weight of my *new* responsibilities towards you that I forget you are first and foremost a baby, *our* baby, with all the needs for fun and freedom which should be every baby's birthright.

Let me be thankful for the people who are there to help us all. Your peripatetic teacher who makes the sessions fun for you and unobtrusively shows *me* the best way to give you the most from your play. The doctors and staff at the Nuffield Centre who patiently explain the technicalities and who listen and show us not only how to cope with hearing aids, ear-moulds and the paraphernalia that is essential to you, but also how to sing and play games and who encourage everything *you* try so eagerly to accomplish.

And how grateful I am to those other parents who have learned so much already and seem so willing to talk to a stranger, to offer the benefit of their experiences and, above all, to hold out hope for your, and our, future.

We have a lot to be thankful for, you and I

Your family is on the brink of a whole new world with you. You are one-year-old and already the easiest part is over. Your new-found legs will soon be carrying you on voyages of discovery which, because of your deafness, will each one hold some danger to which I cannot shout a warning. Our home, from being a haven, will become a hazard for a small but intrepid explorer!

You will no longer be a captive audience. At times you may have to be restrained to sit and *watch* what I say. Unless I am very lucky, and your so far sunny nature remains unchanged, there may be tears and tantrums. Will *my* temper stand the strain?

You won't always be a rosy-cheeked cherub with a ready smile, attracting admiring glances in your pram. You may become a very frustrated two-year-old (and who could blame you?) I only hope that those who frown at your possibly noisy vocalisations, myself included, will stop and think how lucky they are that they *can* hear them. But that is in the future . . .

In the meantime, we have a lot to learn, you and I

But He who helped you fight your first big battle will not desert you now and with your determination, our dedication and the experts' guidance, yellow *will* be a lovely word to see, believe me, Thomas.

Appendix 2

A Second Letter to a Deaf Son (written in Spring, 1992 and celebrating a decade of experience)

We have learned a lot, you and I

We have chased language through books, through games, through teachers, through family and friends, through television, so that now you constantly amaze me with your use of English signs and speech. You've been taught new expressions or words and delighted us all by using them immediately in a different but equally correct context. Your learning has been a joy to see and you are allowed some mistakes, like the frustration you have in remembering the name of one of your favourite programmes. I'm sure the lovely Michael Crawford would forgive you your 'Some Mothers Have Do 'Em'!

Despite the concentration required of you, you lip-read well and your signing skills are good. You improvise signs unfamiliar to you and when I am too dense to understand you always think of an alternative way to make your remark or phrase your question, or add extra information to clarify the content.

We have met Deaf people, learned a little of their language (BSL) and culture, been helped to understand their history and background, their hurts, their concerns, their problems and, most important of all, their gifts.

We had a lot to come to terms with, you and I

It is painfully apparent that even with the best aid on the market you will not hear my voice. I observe other deaf children's desolation when their batteries are flat. You have never even noticed yours . . . You have been exposed to noise for years now, but still the only household sound I've seen you turn to is that made as your bath water empties away.

We have so much to be thankful for, you and I

Our confidence has come from being given the right advice at the right time, by the right people. For starting to sign when you were a baby so that you went to nursery school knowing things had names. So you could make your ideas, your wants and your feelings known. The continuing support we have had from teachers and classroom assistants at the Hearing Impairment Units and the relationships so formed have all been to your lasting benefit.

To my mind it was a miracle that you survived meningitis. To see you grow up, profoundly deaf, with an abundance of confidence, good humour and concern for others, to see and hear you use language not only for basic needs but to negotiate, to soothe, to tease, to cajole, to question, to predict is a bonus we never dared dream of eleven years ago. I have come to the conclusion that He who healed a deaf man has ways of making you whole, other than by *hearing*. I feel I have been privileged to have had a hand in this and His help in what I have strived to do.

Appendix 3

Some Useful Addresses

Arrow* Centre (*Aural-Read-Respond-Oral-Written)
Bridgewater College Campus
Bath Road
Bridgewater, Somerset
TA6 4PZ

British Deaf Association (BDA)
1–3 Worship Street,
London
EC2A 2AB
www.bda.org.uk

British Association of Teachers of the Deaf (BATOD)
41 The Orchard
Leven
Beverley
HU17 5QA
www.batod.org.uk

Council for the Advancement of Communication With Deaf People
(CACDP)
National examining board for communication skills
Durham University Science Park, Block 4
Stockton Road
Durham
DH1 3UZ
www.cacdp.org.uk

Cochlear (UK) Ltd.
Mill House
8 Mill Street
London
SE1 2BA

Cochlear Implanted Children's Support (CICS) Group
Tricia Kemp
4 Ranelagh Avenue
Barnes
London
SW13 0BY

Friends for Young Deaf People (FYD)
East Court Mansion (Head Office)
College Lane
East Grinstead
West Sussex
www.fyd.org.uk

The Forest Book Shop (specialises in books, videos and CD Roms on
deafness and deaf issues)
8 St. John Street
Coleford
Gloucestershire
GL16 8AR
www.forestbooks.com

LASER (Language and Sign as an Educational Resource)
c/o Miranda Pickersgill
Blenheim Centre
Crowther Place
Leeds
LS6 2ST

The Meningitis Research Foundation
Midland Way
Thornbury
Bristol
BS35 2BS
www.meningitis.org

The Meningitis Trust
Fern House
Bath Road
Stroud
Gloucestershire
GL5 3TJ
www.meningitis-trust.org.uk

The National Cochlear Implant Users' Association (NCIUA)
P.O. Box 260
High Wycombe
Bucks
HP11 1FA
www.nciua.demon.co.uk

The National Deaf Children's Society
15 Dufferin Street
London
EC1Y 8UR
www.ndcs.org.uk

Paget Gorman Society
2 Downlands Bungalows
Downloads Lane
Smallfield
Surrey
RH6 9SD
www.pgss.org

The Royal National Institute for Deaf People
19–23 Featherstone Street
London
EC1Y 8SL
www.rnid.org.uk

SENSE (The National Deafblind and Rubella Association)
11–13 Clifton Terrace
Finsbury Park
London
N4 3SR
www.sense.org.uk

SPIT (Signed Performances in Theatre)
1 Stobart Avenue
Manchester
M25 0AJ
www.spit.org.uk

Working Party for Signed English (WPSE),
c/o David Baker
20 Magdalen Road
Exeter
EX2 4TD

Appendix 4

Glossary

BSL	British Sign Language – the first or preferred language of an estimated 50,000 Deaf people in the UK and the language of the Deaf community. It is a visual-gestural/spatial language governed by its own grammar rules and principles which are completely different from the grammatical rules of English.
CACDP	Council for the Advancement of Communication with Deaf People. The awarding body for a number of qualifications that indicate a person's communicative competence in BSL.
Cochlear implant	Device implanted into the cochlea which aims to stimulate the auditory nerve electronically.
FYD	Friends For Young Deaf People – a charity linking deaf, hard-of-hearing and hearing people, using all methods of communication.
HIU	Hearing Impairment Unit (usually part of a mainstream school).
NCT	National Childbirth Trust
NDCS	National Deaf Children's Society
PGSS	Paget Gorman Signed Speech – a grammatical sign system which reflects normal patterns of English.
RNID	The Royal National Institute for Deaf People
SE	Signed English – a system which uses traditional and generated signs with the intention of showing grammatical features of English which may not otherwise be perceivable to a child through either listening or lip-reading.

SSE   Sign Supported English – use of signs borrowed
                        from BSL to support the spoken form of English.
TC   Total communication (an educational approach
                        where all modes of communication are considered)

References

Acredolo, L. and Goodwyn, S. (1996) *Baby Signs*. London: Hodder & Stoughton.

Ashley, J. (1973) *Journey into Silence*. London: Bodley Head.

Batchelor, M. compiled (1992) *Prayer from Mozarabic Sacramentary*. The Lion Prayer Collection. London: Lion Publishing.

Bellitz, S.J. (1983) Thoughts of a deaf child. *The Florida School Herald*.

Berenstain, S. and J. (1972) *Bears in the Night*. London: Collins Harvill.

Bertling, T. (1994) *A Child Sacrificed to the Deaf Culture*. Oregon: Kodiak Media Group.

Berg, L. (1977) *Reading and Loving*. London: Routledge & Kegan Paul.

Bloom, F. (1978) *Our Deaf Children into the 80's*. London: Gresham Books.

Bombeck, E. (1983) *Motherhood – The Second Oldest Profession*. New York: McGraw Hill.

Clark, G. (2000) *Sounds from Silence: The Bionic Ear Story*. St Leonards, NSW, Australia: Allen & Unwin.

Courtman-Davies, M. (1979) *Your Deaf Child's Speech and Language*. London: Bodley Head.

Denmark, J.C. (1994) *Deafness and Mental Health*. London: Jessica Kingsley Publishers.

Dowling, D. and J. (1990) *Learning Together ABC, A Finger-Spelling Alphabet with Signs for Deaf and Hearing Children*. Sheffield: Dowling.

Figes, E. (1997) *The Knot*. London: Minerva by Mandarin Paperbacks.

Fletcher, L. (1987) *Language for Ben*. London: Souvenir Press.

Horwood, W. (1987) *Skallagrigg*. London: Viking.

Karmiloff-Smith, A. (1994) *Baby It's You*. London: Channel 4 by Ebury Press.

Kittel, C.P. and R. (1995) Cochlear implant: A family's experience. In *Cochlear Implant and Bilingualism, A Workshop Report* (pp. 29–40). A LASER Publication.

Lively, P. (1987) *Moon Tiger*. London: Allen Lane.

MacNeice, L. (1966) 'Prayer before birth'. *Collected Poems of Louis MacNeice*. London: Faber and Faber.

Marathon Sign Dictionaries and Videos, London Borough of Bromley, available from Sensory Support Service, Widmore Centre, Nightingale Lane, Bromley BR1 2SQ.

Marschark, M. (1993) *Psychological Development of Deaf Children*. New York: Oxford University Press Inc.

Marschark, M. (1997) *Raising and Educating a Deaf Child*. New York: Oxford University Press.

Mellonie, B. and Ingpen, R. (1983) *Beginnings and Endings with LIFETIMES in Between*. Limpsfield, Surrey: Paper Tiger.

National Cochlear Implant Users' Association (2001) *Cochlear Implants: A Collection of Experiences of Users of all Ages*. High Wycombe: NCIUA.

Parsons, J. (1996) Memory – the forgotten cognitive skill: Encouraging the development of memory strategies in signing pupils. *BATOD* 20(4), 101–10.

Roper, M. (1997) 'What the deer said'. *Catching the Light*. Calstock: Peterloo Poets.

Rosie, H. and Gordon, M. (1999) *My Island – The True Story of a Silent Challenge*. Kirkwall: The Orcadian, Kirkwall Press.

Sidransky, R. (1990) *In Silence: Growing up Hearing in a Deaf World*. London: Piatkus.

Stelle, T.W. (1982) *A Primer for Parents with Deaf Children*. Edinburgh: Scottish Workshop Publications.

Taizé, Brother Roger of (1991) *No Greater Love: Sources of Taizé*. London: Geoffrey Chapman Mowbray.

Vanier, J. (1988) *The Broken Body*. London: Darton, Longman and Todd.

Index

amniocentesis 12
Ashley, Jack 1, 101
Atkinson, Wendy 28, 33, 36, 44, 139, 158
Attenborough, David 39

Barry, John 82, 83
BATOD 84
Beckenham Parish Church 6
Bellman, Dr Sue 103, 119
Berg, Leila 31, 36, 37, 51
Bertling, Tom 125, 158
Bloom, Freddy 20
Bombeck, Erma 45
British Deaf Association 102
British Sign Language 28, 32, 34, 37, 54, 89, 131, 132, 157, 158,
Bromley Chain 49, 58, 83, 94, 95, 96, 143, 156

Carpenter, Canon Derek 109, 110, 111, 116, 137
Chomsky, Noam 130
Clark, Professor Graeme 123, 124
Clements, Michele 10
cochlear implant 62, 98, 99, 100, 101, 103, 104, 108, 113, 114, 118, 121, 123, 124, 125, 142, 163
Conway, Rev'd Steffen, 40, 85, 148
Courtman-Davies, Mary 56

Darrick Wood Schools 39, 46, 50, 73, 78, 80, 91
Deaf Drama Club 63, 67, 85
Denmark, John 162
Disability Living Allowance 41, 153
Douglas, Jane 132
Dowling, Dorothy 23, 59

Egan, Dawn 109
epilepsy 66, 69, 71, 73, 75, 76, 86, 100, 103, 161

Farnborough Hospital 2, 10, 39, 48, 68, 71, 105
Figes, Eva 129
Fletcher, Lorraine 129
FYD 61, 89, 90, 91, 123, 141

Gallagher, Pam 132
Good Housekeeping 1, 39
Graham, Ray Harrison 40, 87
Great Ormond Street Hospital 100, 101, 103, 104, 110, 116, 118, 119, 120, 126
Guy's Hospital 8, 9, 13, 66, 68, 69, 71, 99, 100, 101

Hearing Impairment Unit 22, 27, 39, 52, 73, 78, 92, 99, 100, 102,
Home and Family 146
Hurd, John 17, 18, 22, 23, 25, 27, 33, 38, 39, 40, 42, 43, 49, 68, 73, 78, 85, 94, 149, 166

Kemp, Tricia 101, 124, 125
Kittel, Piers 102, 105

Lively, Penelope 128

MacNeice, Louis 13
Marathon Sign Dictionaries 54
Marcus, Gary 130
Marschark, Marc 26, 128, 131, 132, 133, 141, 162
meningitis 1, 2, 4, 15, 34, 51, 99, 111, 132

NCT 36, 145
NDCS 20, 72, 73, 78, 99, 102
National Hospital for Nervous Diseases 14, 18
Nuffield Centre 18,19, 20, 22, 25, 26, 30, 42, 45, 48, 100, 127, 165

Observer 114, 130

One in Seven 59, 109

PGSS 27, 28, 37, 41, 45, 54
Parsons, Jackie 78, 80, 84, 85, 100, 113,
    120, 121, 123, 161

Regan, John 118
Rosie, Hamish 51
RNID 23, 59
RNTNE Hospital 18, 126

St George's Church, Beckenham 9,
    59, 67, 75, 85, 88, 89, 94, 109, 110,
    116, 137, 138, 145, 148
Saville, Canon Jeremy 12, 30
Scott, Sarah 40, 63, 77, 87
Sense (National Deafblind and
    Rubella Association) 145, 146, 150
signing 23, 24, 25, 26, 27, 30, 35, 64,
    76, 84, 86, 154

Signed English 28, 34, 37, 54, 59, 131,
    132, 133, 143
Sign Supported English 34, 84, 89,
    131, 133, 143,157
Silk, Rev'd David 6, 7, 85, 86
Stelle, Truman 130
Streisand, Barbra 9
Sydenham Children's Hospital 5, 68

Taize, Brother Roger of 71

UCL Adult Cochlear Implant
    Programme 101, 126

Vanier, Jean 118, 177
Video Memory 84

Winston, Roy 40
Woman's Weekly 1, 94, 118
Worth, Jill 146